PANCHO VILLA

PANCHO VILLA

Steven O'Brien

CHELSEA HOUSE PUBLISHERS

NEW YORK ■ PHILADELPHIA

CHELSEA HOUSE PUBLISHERS

Editorial Director: Richard Rennert
Executive Managing Editor: Karyn Gullen Browne
Copy Chief: Robin James
Picture Editor: Adrian G. Allen
Art Director: Robert Mitchell
Manufacturing Director: Gerald Levine
Production Coordinator: Marie Claire Cebrián-Ume

HISPANICS OF ACHIEVEMENT
Senior Editor: Philip Koslow

Staff for PANCHO VILLA
Assistant Editor: David C. Carter
Designer: M. Cambraia Magalhães
Picture Researchers: Toby Greenberg, Sandy Jones

3 5 7 9 8 6 4 2

Library of Congress Cataloging-in-Publication Data
O'Brien, Steven.
Pancho Villa/Steven O'Brien.
p. cm.—(Hispanics of achievement)
Includes bibliographical references and index.
ISBN 0-7910-1257-3
0-7910-1284-0 (pbk.)
1. Villa, Pancho, 1878–1923—Juvenile literature. 2. Mexico—History—Revolution, 1910–1920—Juvenile literature. [1. Villa, Pancho, 1878–1923. 2. Revolutionaries. 3. Mexico—History—Revolution, 1910–1920.] I. Title. II. Series.
93-37890
F1234.V7503 1994
CIP
972.08'092—dc20
AC

CONTENTS

JOAN BAEZ
Mexican-American folksinger

RUBÉN BLADES
Panamanian lawyer and entertainer

JORGE LUIS BORGES
Argentine writer

PABLO CASALS
Spanish cellist and conductor

MIGUEL DE CERVANTES
Spanish writer

CESAR CHAVEZ
Mexican-American labor leader

JULIO CÉSAR CHÁVEZ
Mexican boxing champion

EL CID
Spanish military leader

HENRY CISNEROS
Mexican-American political leader

ROBERTO CLEMENTE
Puerto Rican baseball player

SALVADOR DALÍ
Spanish painter

PLÁCIDO DOMINGO
Spanish singer

GLORIA ESTEFAN
Cuban-American singer

GABRIEL GARCÍA MÁRQUEZ
Colombian writer

FRANCISCO JOSÉ DE GOYA
Spanish painter

JULIO IGLESIAS
Spanish singer

RAUL JULIA
Puerto Rican actor

FRIDA KAHLO
Mexican painter

JOSÉ MARTÍ
Cuban revolutionary and poet

RITA MORENO
Puerto Rican singer and actress

PABLO NERUDA
Chilean poet and diplomat

OCTAVIO PAZ
Mexican poet and critic

PABLO PICASSO
Spanish artist

ANTHONY QUINN
Mexican-American actor

DIEGO RIVERA
Mexican painter

LINDA RONSTADT
Mexican-American singer

ANTONIO LÓPEZ DE SANTA ANNA
Mexican general and politician

GEORGE SANTAYANA
Spanish philosopher and poet

JUNÍPERO SERRA
Spanish missionary and explorer

LEE TREVINO
Mexican-American golfer

PANCHO VILLA
Mexican revolutionary

CHELSEA HOUSE PUBLISHERS

HISPANICS OF ACHIEVEMENT

Rodolfo Cardona

The Spanish language and many other elements of Spanish culture are present in the United States today and have been since the country's earliest beginnings. Some of these elements have come directly from the Iberian Peninsula; others have come indirectly, by way of Mexico, the Caribbean basin, and the countries of Central and South America.

Spanish culture has influenced America in many subtle ways, and consequently many Americans remain relatively unaware of the extent of its impact. The vast majority of them recognize the influence of Spanish culture in America, but they often do not realize the great importance and long history of that influence. This is partly because Americans have tended to judge the Hispanic influence in the United States in statistical terms rather than to look closely at the ways in which individual Hispanics have profoundly affected American culture. For this reason, it is fitting that Americans obtain more than a passing acquaintance with the origins of these Spanish cultural elements and gain an understanding of how they have been woven into the fabric of American society.

It is well documented that Spanish seafarers were the first to explore and colonize many of the early territories of what is today called the United States of America. For this reason, students of geography discover Hispanic names all over the map of the United States. For instance, the Strait of Juan de Fuca was named after the Spanish explorer who first navigated the waters of the Pacific Northwest; the names of states such as Arizona (arid zone), Montana (mountain), Florida (thus named because it was reached on Easter Sunday, which in Spanish is called the feast of Pascua Florida), and California (named after a fictitious land in one of the first and probably the most popular among the Spanish novels of chivalry, *Amadis of Gaul*) are all derived from Spanish; and there are numerous mountains, rivers, canyons, towns, and cities with Spanish names throughout the United States.

Not only explorers but many other illustrious figures in Spanish history have helped define American culture. For example, the 13th-century king of Spain, Alfonso X, also known as the Learned, may be unknown to the majority of Americans, but his work on the codification of Spanish law has greatly influenced the evolution of American law, particularly in the jurisdictions of the Southwest. For this contribution a statue of him stands in the rotunda of the Capitol in Washington, D.C. Likewise, the name Diego Rivera may be unfamiliar to most Americans, but this Mexican painter influenced many American artists whose paintings, commissioned during the Great Depression and the New Deal era of the 1930s, adorn the walls of government buildings throughout the United States. In recent years the contributions of Puerto Ricans, Mexicans, Mexican Americans (Chicanos), and Cubans in American cities such as Boston, Chicago, Los Angeles, Miami, Minneapolis, New York, and San Antonio have been enormous.

The importance of the Spanish language in this vast cultural complex cannot be overstated. Spanish, after all, is second only to English as the most widely spoken of Western languages within the United States as well as in the entire world. The popularity of the Spanish language in America has a long history.

In addition to Spanish exploration of the New World, the great Spanish literary tradition served as a vehicle for bringing the language and culture to America. Interest in Spanish literature in America began when English immigrants brought with them translations of Spanish masterpieces of the Golden Age. As early as 1683, private libraries in Philadelphia and Boston contained copies of the first picaresque novel, *Lazarillo de Tormes*, translations of Francisco de Quevedo's *Los Sueños*, and copies of the immortal epic of reality and illusion *Don Quixote*, by the great Spanish writer Miguel de Cervantes. It would not be surprising if Cotton Mather, the arch-Puritan, read *Don Quixote* in its original Spanish, if only to enrich his vocabulary in preparation for his writing *La fe del cristiano en 24 artículos de la Institución de Cristo, enviada a los españoles para que abran sus ojos* (The Christian's Faith in 24 Articles of the Institution of Christ, Sent to the Spaniards to Open Their Eyes), published in Boston in 1699.

Over the years, Spanish authors and their works have had a vast influence on American literature—from Washington Irving, John Steinbeck, and Ernest Hemingway in the novel to Henry Wadsworth Longfellow and Archibald MacLeish in poetry. Such important American writers as James Fenimore Cooper, Edgar Allan Poe, Walt Whitman, Mark Twain, and Herman Melville all owe a sizable debt to the Spanish literary tradition. Some writers, such as Willa Cather and Maxwell Anderson, who explored Spanish themes they came into contact with in the American Southwest and Mexico, were influenced less directly but no less profoundly.

Important contributions to a knowledge of Spanish culture in the United States were also made by many lesser known individuals—teachers, publishers, historians, entrepreneurs, and others—with a love for Spanish culture. One of the most significant of these contributions was made by Abiel Smith, a Harvard College graduate of the class of 1764, when he bequeathed stock worth $20,000 to Harvard for the support of a professor of French and Spanish. By 1819 this endowment had produced enough income to appoint a professor, and the philologist and humanist George Ticknor became the first holder of the Abiel

Smith Chair, which was the very first endowed Chair at Harvard University. Other illustrious holders of the Smith Chair would include the poets Henry Wadsworth Longfellow and James Russell Lowell.

A highly respected teacher and scholar, Ticknor was also a collector of Spanish books, and as such he made a very special contribution to America's knowledge of Spanish culture. He was instrumental in amassing for Harvard libraries one of the first and most impressive collections of Spanish books in the United States. He also had a valuable personal collection of Spanish books and manuscripts, which he bequeathed to the Boston Public Library.

With the creation of the Abiel Smith Chair, Spanish language and literature courses became part of the curriculum at Harvard, which also went on to become the first American university to offer graduate studies in Romance languages. Other colleges and universities throughout the United States gradually followed Harvard's example, and today Spanish language and culture may be studied at most American institutions of higher learning.

No discussion of the Spanish influence in the United States, however brief, would be complete without a mention of the Spanish influence on art. Important American artists such as John Singer Sargent, James A. M. Whistler, Thomas Eakins, and Mary Cassatt all explored Spanish subjects and experimented with Spanish techniques. Virtually every serious American artist living today has studied the work of the Spanish masters as well as the great 20th-century Spanish painters Salvador Dalí, Joan Miró, and Pablo Picasso.

The most pervasive Spanish influence in America, however, has probably been in music. Compositions such as Leonard Bernstein's *West Side Story*, the Latinization of William Shakespeare's *Romeo and Juliet* set in New York's Puerto Rican quarter, and Aaron Copland's *Salon Mexico* are two obvious examples. In general, one can hear the influence of Latin rhythms—from tango to mambo, from guaracha to salsa—in virtually every form of American music.

This series of biographies, which Chelsea House has published under the general title HISPANICS OF ACHIEVEMENT, constitutes further recognition of—and a renewed effort to bring forth to the consciousness of America's young people—the contributions that Hispanic people have made not only in the United States but throughout the civilized world. The men and women who are featured in this series have attained a high level of accomplishment in their respective fields of endeavor and have made a permanent mark on American society.

The title of this series must be understood in its broadest possible sense: The term *Hispanics* is intended to include Spaniards, Spanish Americans, and individuals from many countries whose language and culture have either direct or indirect Spanish origins. The names of many of the people included in this series will be immediately familiar; others will be less recognizable. All, however, have attained recognition within their own countries, and often their fame has transcended their borders.

The series HISPANICS OF ACHIEVEMENT thus addresses the attainments and struggles of Hispanic people in the United States and seeks to tell the stories of individuals whose personal and professional lives in some way reflect the larger Hispanic experience. These stories are exemplary of what human beings can accomplish, often against daunting odds and by extraordinary personal sacrifice, where there is conviction and determination. Fray Junípero Serra, the 18th-century Spanish Franciscan missionary, is one such individual. Although in very poor health, he devoted the last 15 years of his life to the foundation of missions throughout California—then a mostly unsettled expanse of land—in an effort to bring a better life to Native Americans through the cultivation of crafts and animal husbandry. An example from recent times, the Mexican-American labor leader Cesar Chavez battled bitter opposition and made untold personal sacrifices in his effort to help poor agricultural workers who have been exploited for decades on farms throughout the Southwest.

The talent with which each one of these men and women may have been endowed required dedication and hard work to develop and become fully realized. Many of them have enjoyed rewards for their efforts during their own lifetime, whereas others have died poor and unrecognized. For some it took a long time to achieve their goals, for others success came at an early age, and for still others the struggle continues. All of them, however, stand out as people whose lives have made a difference, whose achievements we need to recognize today and should continue to honor in the future.

PANCHO VILLA

CHAPTER
ONE

DESPERADO

T hree days of fierce but inconclusive fighting in
early November 1913 left Mexican revolutionary
Pancho Villa with little choice. He had to order a halt
to his attack upon Chihuahua City. The Federal Army
troops defending Chihuahua were too well armed and
dug in for his rebel Division of the North to dislodge.

As soon as federal reconnaissance patrols reported
that all of Villa's troops had left the Chihuahua area,
Mexican dictator Victoriano Huerta's generals breathed
a collective sigh of relief. Obviously, Villa's desperate
gamble to regain his status as a major rebel leader by
taking Chihuahua had failed. Now, they thought, it
would just be a matter of time before he was captured
and executed.

With the threat of attack by Villa's forces gone, life
in northern Mexico quickly returned to normal. Mes-
sages shuttled over the telegraph wires once again, and
regular train service resumed.

But the reports of Villa's demise were premature.
His decision to order a retreat into the desert did not
mean that he was beaten. When his agents intercepted
a telegraph message detailing the schedule of a coal
train heading south from Ciudad Juárez, Mexico's
most important border town, Villa realized that fate

Francisco "Pancho" Villa, photographed during the early years of the Mexican Revolution, when he commanded rebel forces in northern Mexico. A villain to some and a hero to others, Villa made an indelible mark on Mexican history and folklore.

15

had given him an opportunity he could not afford to miss. He quickly formulated a bold plan to turn his opponents' overconfidence to his own advantage. The potential for catastrophe was tremendous, but Villa did not hesitate. He knew that he had to accept whatever risks were necessary to regain the initiative.

In a matter of hours, Villa had selected 2,000 of his best troops to go with him, and this small army began a forced march across the desert to a strategic site south of Ciudad Juárez where the railroad passed.

Orchestrating the ambush of a train was a simple affair for the former train robber. A barricade was thrown across the tracks in a narrow gorge, and when the train halted, Villa and his men swooped down from the canyons and overpowered the military escort on board. When the commandeered train made its last refueling stop before Chihuahua, the rebels seized the station's telegraph office.

Villa's men put a gun to the telegraph operator's head and ordered him to tap out a message to Juárez. They indicated that one of their number knew the telegraph code and that any attempt to warn the garrisons at Juárez or Chihuahua would result in a quick death. Villa ordered the following message sent: DERAILED. NO LINE TO CHIHUAHUA. EVERYTHING BURNED BY REVOLUTIONARIES. SEND SECOND EN- GINE AND ORDERS. After a few tense moments, the reply came from Ciudad Juárez: NO ENGINES. FIND TOOLS. ADVISE AND WAIT FOR ORDERS WHEN BACK ON RAILS.

Within two hours, the train had been emptied of its load of coal and now held a very different freight, 2,000 of Villa's revolutionaries. Villa then ordered the telegrapher to send a second wire: ON TRACKS. NO ROAD OR WIRE SOUTH. BIG CLOUD OF DUST—PER- HAPS REVOLUTIONARIES. Immediately the wires were humming with the response: BACK INTO JUÁREZ.

Villa and some of his officers pose in full battle dress. Villa's daring military tactics, developed during his years as a bandit leader, enabled his rebel Division of the North to defeat more numerous and better-armed government forces in 1913.

WIRE AT EACH STATION. Villa ordered his men to cut the telegraph line so that no warning could be sent after the revolutionaries had left. Other men quickly tore up the tracks to the south to prevent pursuit from Chihuahua.

As the train reached each station on its way north, telegraph operators were forced to send the required "all clear" signals to Juárez. When the rebels neared the city, Villa placed several soldiers and one of his railroad men in the train's engine cab and issued strict orders: If the engineer tried to stop before reaching the station, "kill him, take the controls, and keep the train moving."

Four hours after Villa had seized the train, it penetrated into the heart of the heavily fortified city with its deadly cargo undetected. Before any alarm could be sounded, the rebels silently streamed from the railway cars and fanned out to capture Juárez's strategic positions.

The surprise was complete. The 4,000 federal troops, fast asleep when Villa's train rumbled into the city, were so shocked by the rebel assault that by dawn on November 15 Villa's men had either killed, captured, or driven to flight virtually the entire garrison.

Villa had captured the most important city on the Mexican–United States border without the loss of even one of his own men. Impressive as this feat was for its daring alone, the wily revolutionary leader had taken Ciudad Juárez for an important strategic reason: it was the lifeline to Chihuahua, the only significant holdout of the Mexican government in the north. If Villa could keep control of the rail link between the two cities, he could make a giant contribution to the Mexican Revolution by driving the reactionary federal government out of northern Mexico.

Apparently Villa's enemies shared his view of the situation. Within days of his capture of Ciudad Juárez, Villa learned that 11 trainloads of federal troops were headed north from Chihuahua City at full throttle. Villa turned to one of his most trusted commanders, Rodolfo Fierro, and instructed him to gain the rebels a day's time no matter the cost. Fierro left immediately with a detachment and returned in only a few hours to announce his success. Even though they were in range of the federal artillery, Fierro and his men had put the rail line out of commission. As an extra flourish, they had left 10 railcars burning on the tracks.

The following day, Villa and his army departed to battle the federal forces. This time, the rebel leader had

Rebel soldiers firing on government forces during the Battle of Juárez in November 1913. After entering Juárez stealthily by train while the Federal Army garrison was asleep, Villa's troops quickly gained control of the vital city and soon moved on to conquer Chihuahua.

more than strictly military worries on his mind. In a 1911 battle at Ciudad Juárez, the fighting had spilled over the border into El Paso, Texas, angering the local citizens. To prevent a recurrence of ruffled feathers in the United States, Villa met with El Paso's mayor immediately after seizing control of Ciudad Juárez and promised to avoid any repetition of the previous incident.

Characteristically, Villa turned this diplomatic problem to his benefit. On November 16, he ordered an impressive review of his troops, for the dual purpose of celebrating the anniversary of the Mexican Revolution and of assuring the El Pasoans that he had everything under control. When the review was over, Villa's troops did not return to the barracks as expected; instead, they clambered aboard waiting trains and headed south. Villa had already decided to meet the oncoming federal forces at Tierra Blanca, 35 miles

south of Juárez. He planned to occupy the high ground, forcing his enemies to fight on sandy terrain that would immobilize their artillery and deprive them of water.

When the two armies met at Tierra Blanca, Villa's opponents understood that he had lured them into a trap. At first they did not attack, perhaps hoping that Villa would abandon his superior position and fight on their ground. When Villa did not oblige them, they were forced to attack his right flank on November 22,

Villa's forces prepare to board a train in November 1913. As a former train robber, Villa knew the ins and outs of the Mexican railway system. His ability to move troops and supplies swiftly by train enabled him to conquer northern Mexico for the revolution.

hoping to seize the Bauche railway station and its all-important water towers. A pitched battle ensued, but Villa's forces held their ground.

The following day, November 23, the federals attacked Villa's left flank and again failed to break through. While their water supplies continued to dwindle, Villa's troops were benefiting from their commander's keen appreciation of the military use of railroads; they received not only water but food and medicine from Ciudad Juárez. By November 25, the battle was raging over such a long front that it nearly reached the Texas border. The federal troops launched a final, desperate attempt to break Villa's lines and were soon on the verge of success. At the moment of crisis, Villa decided to employ one of his favorite maneuvers: a massed cavalry charge into the enemy's center. He informed his officers that the signal for the attack would be the firing of two cannons.

When the cannon shots shattered the heated air above Tierra Blanca, the rebels' swift cavalry tore into the federal lines like a fire sweeping through a wheat field. Panicked soldiers fled the field and tried to escape to Chihuahua by train. Many got away, but some were not so lucky. One of the trains was intercepted by the formidable Rodolfo Fierro: he jumped aboard from his galloping horse, climbed along the roofs of the cars until he reached the brake cylinder, and engaged the brakes, bringing the train to a grinding halt. Villa's troops fell upon the train's occupants, and it was said that Villa himself admitted that a terrible slaughter took place.

After Tierra Blanca, it was a foregone conclusion that Villa would finally take Chihuahua City and command the north of Mexico for the revolution. Remarkably, only a little more than eight months earlier, Villa had crossed the border from Texas with only eight followers. His only purpose then was to avenge the murder of his hero, Mexican president Francisco Madero, and to help salvage the Mexican Revolution. The man who had once been a humble peasant and then an infamous bandit succeeded so well that by the time he reached Tierra Blanca, one influential magazine in the United States had called the entire revolution "Villa's uprising."

Because of his amazing triumphs against long odds, people in Mexico's northern states of Chihuahua, Durango, and Sonora still tell stories about the exploits of Pancho Villa. On the northern side of the Rio Grande, he is more often remembered as a cut-throat.

Both views contain elements of truth. Pancho Villa was capable of gross self-indulgence and patriotic self-sacrifice, brutal mayhem, and deep generosity. In order to make sense of the warring impulses of his nature, it is necessary to understand the violent world that shaped him.

BANDIT PATRIOT

Pancho Villa in his early twenties, shortly after assuming his command as a general in the revolutionary army. A bandit since the age of 16, Villa found in the Mexican Revolution an outlet for his lifelong hatred of Mexico's wealthy landowners.

Francisco "Pancho" Villa was born in the small village of Rio Grande in the northern Mexican state of Durango on June 5, 1878. He was given the baptismal name of Doroteo Arango. Doroteo's parents, Augustín Arango and María Micaela Arambula, were illiterate farmers who toiled from dawn to dusk on a huge estate known as the Hacienda del Rio Grande.

Doroteo's formal education consisted only of the rudiments of reading and writing, which he learned in the small, church-run village school. Starting at the age of seven, when his father died, he had to help care for his younger brothers and sisters. By age 11, he had managed to combine his love of horses with his need to supplement the meager family income; he obtained work as a helper to wagon drivers. This job enabled him to escape the confines of his isolated rural village. More important for the future bandit and revolutionary leader, it also gave him an intimate knowledge of the desert and mountain terrain of northern Mexico.

Doroteo was a popular and well-respected teenager in his village, but he was too strong-willed and industrious to meekly accept the humble life of an impoverished peon, or day laborer. When an opportunity arose to earn more money by working at the Hacienda del Norte, he accepted it without obtaining permission from the owner of the Hacienda del Rio Grande.

Doroteo's action was against the law. The punishment for such independent behavior by a peon in 19th-century Mexico was savage. Doroteo was captured, bound, and forced to run barefoot behind a horse all the way back from the Hacienda del Norte. Then, in the main square of Rio Grande, he was brutally flogged. The excruciating pain and humiliation he suffered for trying to improve his lot in life only intensified the boy's rebellious spirit. He began to associate with the leader of a group of young men suspected of being cattle thieves. After another failed attempt to escape from the hacienda, he was convicted of being an accomplice in the theft and butchering of a stolen steer. After a quick trial, the 16-year-old Doroteo was sentenced to prison.

Doroteo was released after a few months, thanks to the efforts of a neighboring hacienda owner. But the experience of living in a grimy cell among hardened criminals had a profound effect on him. Instead of returning directly to his village, Doroteo obtained menial work in Chihuahua City. He also apparently cultivated underworld contacts acquired in prison. In order to earn extra money, he passed them information he obtained on gold shipments and cattle drives.

The money he earned in Chihuahua enabled Doroteo to help support his family. He also had enough time and money to court a young Indian girl named María Luz Corral. They fell in love and became engaged.

Doroteo might have spent the rest of his life as a laborer and petty criminal if he had not felt obliged to avenge the honor of his youngest sister. When he learned that the son of a hacienda owner had seduced and abandoned her, he confronted the man and shot him dead. The punishment for attacking a member of the aristocracy, regardless of the provocation, was death.

Mexican peons plow the fields in the early 20th century, using methods dating back more than 1,000 years. Villa was born into this hardworking, exploited rural class, but his rebellious nature drove him to become a bold and ruthless outlaw.

Doroteo had no alternative but to steal the fastest horse available and flee to the remote mountains known as the Sierra Madre.

Against all odds, the young fugitive managed to elude the police patrols sent to catch him. He had already learned from experience to cover his tracks and preserve the strength of his horse by avoiding the temptation to make a mad dash for freedom. The teenager knew the best hiding places in the rough mountain terrain, the type of cactus to cut open for badly needed moisture, and the art of making silent traps to catch wild rabbits and armadillos, which he could eat raw for nourishment.

One morning, after spending the night next to a stream in a verdant canyon of the Barranca del Cobre, Doroteo awoke with a start. Staring down at him was the infamous outlaw Ignacio Parra. Parra was the man the boy had hoped to meet, but he had to rely upon his wits to gain the right to join his gang. To prove his potential value, he drew maps in the sand that illus- trated the different grazing locations of several of the largest cattle herds in the region. Parra was so im-

pressed by the stamina and cleverness Doroteo had
shown in escaping from the police that he decided to
take a chance on him. Within a few months, the
youngster was a fully accepted member of Parra's
gang.

Along with his new life, Doroteo chose a new
name—Francisco "Pancho" Villa. (In Mexico, Pancho
is the common nickname for Francisco.) The original
Pancho Villa had been a well-known bandit leader
who, according to legend, robbed from the rich and
gave to the poor. Doroteo was sure he was destined to
fulfill the same role. He had a distant relative named
Jesús Villa, and he believed that this established his link
to the legendary bandit.

Doroteo had not only changed his name. He had
grown into a barrel-chested man with curly, reddish
brown hair. He grew a bushy mustache to hide the
uneven, protruding teeth that gave him the appearance of wearing a perpetual smile. Wide in the shoul-
ders and six feet tall, he was strikingly larger than most
of his fellow Mexicans.

Villa was generally quiet and self-disciplined, but
he had a violent temper and could explode at the
slightest provocation. Any man who frustrated his
desires, deceived him, or insulted him was lucky to
escape with only a severe beating. Villa never forgot a
betrayal and always obtained revenge.

After joining Parra's gang, Villa took part in many
robberies and hacienda raids and rustled numerous
head of cattle. In addition to becoming a ruthless
criminal capable of killing and torturing without re-
morse, he learned how to be a skillful rider, marksman,
and tactician. Villa's remarkable ability to lead and to
inspire loyalty first emerged among the bandits of
Chihuahua.

In the usual raiding technique employed by Parra,
the bandits crept close to their target in the dead of
night. At dawn, they pounced amid a storm of scream-

ing and shooting. When everything worked according to plan, the victims were stripped of their merchandise and personal wealth in a matter of minutes. Then the desperados dashed back into the Sierra Madre canyons, losing the pursuing police in the rugged mountain terrain.

One day, government troops lured the bandits into attacking a decoy payroll wagon and then sprang a deadly trap. Parra was cut down in a hail of gunfire, and the leaderless bandits began to panic. Villa saved the day by rallying the survivors and leading a desperate charge that enabled them to escape.

Back at their hideout, the decimated group formally accepted Villa as Parra's successor. Villa quickly came up with a new operating procedure for the gang. Those who were not known to the police were ordered to return to regular civilian life. Meanwhile, Villa and a small corps of men remained in the mountains to collect intelligence and plan raids. When the time to strike was near, a rider was sent out in the night. The shout "¡Viva Villa!"—accompanied by a dagger stuck into the door of a man's adobe home—was the summons to appear at a prearranged location, ready to participate in a raid.

Unlike some of his cohorts, Villa was not a career criminal. In the years between his entry into Parra's gang and the outbreak of the revolution in 1910, he made several attempts to rejoin normal society. Once, for a brief period of time, he worked as a laborer in southern Arizona and New Mexico. In 1903, he accepted the opportunity to earn an amnesty by "volunteering" to serve in the 14th Cavalry Regiment. When he and María Luz Corral were legally married in 1909, he purchased a large, comfortable house in Chihuahua City.

Despite Villa's periodic desire to settle down, the life of a bandit leader proved too exciting and lucrative to exchange for domestic tranquility. Only by living outside the law could Villa indulge his passion for women without regard for traditional social conventions. In addition to María Luz, he married at least two other women, Soledad Seáñez and Estroberta Rentería, maintained numerous lovers, and had countless brief liaisons.

Villa loved to sing and dance. Whenever possible, he visited cantinas, smoking, and nursing a single drink while joining in choruses of popular songs and dancing till dawn—preferably with a new woman who had just caught his fancy.

To a large extent, social conditions in late-19th-century Mexico drove men such as Villa into banditry. In Mexico, as in the United States, this was the age of the robber baron. A "survival of the fittest" mentality prevailed, unchecked by any thought of sharing the national wealth with those less able to compete. Small farmers and ranchers were being systematically driven out of business and into virtual slavery by the economic policies of Porfirio Díaz, Mexico's dictator.

Díaz ruled Mexico, with one brief interruption, from 1877 to 1911. His principal policy was to bring foreign investment into Mexico. Huge tracts of land, mining companies, banks, and the railroads were soon owned by Europeans and North Americans. Money flowed into the country, but the wealth gained by a tiny minority of Mexicans never trickled down to the vast majority of the population.

Díaz abolished the few traditional safeguards that had controlled the greed of the wealthy. The small landowner became a thing of the past. Instead, absentee landlords acquired immense estates and hired managers to run them, with the single goal of earning as much profit as possible.

Díaz's dreaded police, known as the Rurales, employed brutality and terror to control the population. The Rurales, originally recruited from among captured bandits who were granted amnesty for joining

Porfirio Díaz, president of Mexico between 1877 and 1911. An iron-willed dictator, Díaz tried to develop Mexico's economy by catering to wealthy landowners and foreign businessmen. His policies were directly responsible for the Mexican Revolution of 1910.

the force, were authorized to shoot criminals and revolutionaries instead of delivering them to trial. Runaway peons, striking workers, personal enemies, and rivals of local political bosses were all likely to be executed for "trying to escape." Anything the Rurales could not handle, the army was called in to settle. Díaz kept the loyalty of the army officers and church officials through bribes and grants of special privileges.

In this atmosphere, men of humble origins who resorted to crime were perceived by the masses as heroes fighting oppression. Numerous ballads and folktales sprang up about Villa. These songs and mythical anecdotes exaggerated his feats of banditry and main-

During his presidency, Díaz created the Rurales, shown here with a group of slain rebels, in order to terrorize the peasants and crush his political opponents. The heavily armed Rurales were the scourge of the Mexican countryside, but they could never capture the bandit leader Pancho Villa.

tained that he, like his namesake, aided the poor with spoils from the rich.

Villa's life prior to 1910 provided a perfect apprenticeship for the role of a successful guerrilla fighter. Planning and executing train robberies, looting banks, and raiding haciendas forced him to become adept at living off the land, avoiding pursuers, controlling unruly men, and coordinating surprise attacks. All he needed to switch from being a bandit to a patriot was a revolutionary ideology to give focus to his anger, and a leader that he could follow. In the summer and fall of 1910, he found his inspiration.

In 1908, Díaz told an American journalist that Mexico was ready for democracy. This statement caused a surge of political activity by the anti-Díaz forces. *The Presidential Succession in 1910,* a book by Francisco Indalécio Madero, became immensely successful. It called for honest elections in 1910, democratic institutions at all levels of government, and the defeat of Díaz. In addition to his eloquent political writing, the idealistic Madero also tried to organize all the different groups opposed to Díaz's continued rule into an Antireelectionist party.

During their brief opportunity to campaign in the summer of 1910, Madero and the Antireelectionist candidate for vice-president, Abrán González, discreetly met with Villa in Chihuahua City to explain their goals and the role Villa could play if their election were prevented by Díaz. Villa was living openly in the city in a large house with María Luz and his two-year-old son, despite having recently killed a man in a gunfight.

Madero attracted much more popular support than Díaz had anticipated when he granted him permission to campaign. As soon as it became clear that he might lose the 1910 election, Díaz threw Madero in jail and forced González to flee to the United States.

After he was returned to office in a sham election with no opposition allowed, Díaz released Madero, warning him to remain silent. Instead of accepting defeat, Madero resumed his protests and escaped to San Antonio, Texas, one step ahead of Díaz's assassins. In October 1910, he published the *Plan of San Luis Potosí,* a manifesto that promised a revision of all the laws enacted under the Díaz regime. He declared himself to be the legitimate president of Mexico and called for an armed insurrection to force Díaz out of office. The Mexican Revolution had begun.

The opportunity to escape the life of an outlaw and play a role in shaping the future of Mexico proved irresistible to Villa. On November 15, 1910, leading a group of 15 men, he returned to the mountains he knew so well, not as a bandit but as a captain in the revolutionary army.

The Mexican Revolution was not the result of a single, well-coordinated opposition movement. Instead of one rebellion there were many, in several different parts of Mexico. Each revolt had its own leader, program, and area of control. For a few brief months Madero was the titular head of an umbrella revolutionary organization, but he actually never had firm control over more than a small number of loyal followers.

While Madero struggled to create a national organization, Villa, at the head of 500 men, captured the town of San Andrés and the important rail junction of Camargo. The rules of conduct he imposed in both communities—no looting or raping, the execution of all captured enemy military officers, and the collection of a special tax upon local merchants, along with forced "loans" from foreign mine owners to pay for equipping his army—were those he attempted to follow throughout most of his military career.

In March 1911, the rebel army, with Madero in command, suffered a crushing defeat at the battle of

Francisco Indalecio
Madero (1873–1913)
was a wealthy landowner
who became a social
reformer and the leader of
the anti-Díaz opposition.
Madero's courage and
idealism aroused the
admiration of Villa, who
put himself and his
bandits under Madero's
command in 1910.

Casas Grandes in Chihuahua. Nevertheless, Madero gained Villa's admiration when he continued to fight valiantly after suffering a serious shoulder wound.

After the defeat, Madero assembled all the rebel forces that would still follow him, and Villa reported for duty with more than 800 men. He was given the task of covering the rebels' retreat to the vicinity of Ciudad Juárez.

The battle at Casas Grandes led foreign observers and Díaz's generals to mistakenly conclude that the government had crushed the rebellion. Actually, although Madero's defeat had left him with a much smaller army, he had a more disciplined and better-equipped force than before. He also adopted a more realistic military objective—the capture of the important border city of Ciudad Juárez. Control of Juárez would enable the rebels to gain access to weapons and financing from the United States.

The details of the capture of Juárez on May 10, 1911, are unclear, but the courage, energy, and initiative of Villa were vital ingredients of the decisive victory. He played a major role in developing the plan of attack, led numerous charges during the four days of the battle, and devised a simple strategy for overcoming the federal garrison's seemingly impregnable street barricades. Instead of wasting men in a direct assault on the barricades, Villa—familiar with the vulnerability of wood and adobe buildings to dynamite from his career as a bank robber—ordered his men to plant explosives in the buildings along one side of a barricaded street. In this manner a path was cleared through the houses around the barricades. The outflanked defenders were forced to surrender or fall back to the next barricade and endure the same process there.

When General Juan Navarro, the commander of the federal garrison, surrendered, Madero established a provisional government. Although Villa was promoted to colonel for his performance during the battle, Madero's refusal to allow the execution of the captured enemy officers infuriated him almost as much as did Madero's choice of Giuseppe Garibaldi, grandson of the 19th-century Italian patriot, as a personal bodyguard. Garibaldi was the commander of the American Legion, a group of American and European soldiers of fortune who had joined the rebel army. He and Villa had such a violent argument, one night shortly after the battle, that Villa followed Garibaldi over the Rio Grande into El Paso, Texas, to challenge him to a gunfight. Instead of obtaining satisfaction, Villa suffered the indignity of being disarmed by American officials and escorted back to the Mexican side of the border.

Mexican rebels pose with a homemade cannon in the border city of Juárez. The capture of Juárez in May 1911, after an attack planned and led by Villa, was a major blow to the Díaz regime: control of the city enabled the rebels to obtain weapons and money from the United States.

Pascual Orozco, a rebel officer disappointed because he was not made minister of war in Madero's cabinet, capitalized upon Villa's frustration. He persuaded Villa to join him and several hundred of their most loyal men in complaining directly to Madero. At the meeting in Madero's headquarters, Orozco, to Villa's surprise, demanded that Madero accept their protective custody. Madero refused to be intimidated, even though his headquarters was surrounded by troops loyal to Orozco and Villa. He listened politely to their complaints, expressed sympathy, explained the reasons behind his actions, and promised that in the future, he would remember their service to the revolution.

Villa was satisfied by Madero's response. As soon as he announced that he had not come to the meeting with any intention of usurping Madero's authority, Orozco quickly concurred.

The incident had important long-term effects. Madero's firmness and personal courage during the tense confrontation transformed Villa's feelings toward him from hesitant acceptance to absolute devotion. His feelings toward Orozco turned from indifference to violent hatred. He became convinced that Orozco had tricked him into confronting Madero to create the appearance that Villa was the instigator of what was actually Orozco's mutiny.

The unexpected victory of Madero at Juárez and the successful uprising of the peasant leader Emiliano Zapata in southern Mexico led to the rapid collapse of the Díaz regime. On May 21, 1911, just 11 days after the capture of Juárez, Díaz announced his decision to relinquish the presidency. Several days later, Madero, accompanied by his cabinet officials and military officers, including Villa, arrived in Mexico City to assume control of the nation.

A band of Mexican rebels occupies a stronghold in the mountains of Chihuahua. In the distance, just across the border, is an industrial section of El Paso, Texas. During the 10-year Mexican Revolution, fighting between Mexicans would often spill over into Texas, leading to reprisals by U.S. forces.

The journey to Mexico City marked the first time that Villa had ever traveled by train south of Chihuahua for more than several hours. The magnificent variety of the terrain and the enthusiasm of the cheering throngs who shouted Madero's name at each railway station undoubtedly made a tremendous impression. The days spent in Mexico City enabled Villa to observe the demeanor and manners of the men who were about to determine the fate of millions of Mexicans with speeches and laws instead of guns. He quickly concluded that the life of a government official did not suit him.

Since the fighting appeared over, Villa requested, and was granted, permission to leave the revolutionary army and return to Chihuahua City. In return for his services, he was authorized to confiscate the cattle of Don Luis Terrazas, a Díaz supporter and hacienda owner whom Villa hated with a special passion. Villa needed the steers to supply the meat for several modern, refrigerated butcher shops he planned to open in Chihuahua City. Orozco was appointed military commander in the state of Chihuahua.

For the next several months, Villa was completely engaged in developing his new business. This was one of the few periods of his adult life during which he was, albeit with a lopsided advantage over his competitors, legally employed. To celebrate his good fortune and the birth of a second child, he remarried María Luz in both civil and religious ceremonies and invited hundreds of guests to a gigantic barbecue and reception.

However, he was not fated to be a businessman for long.

THE FUGITIVE

Villa on horseback, photographed during his campaigns of 1913. After the collapse of the Díaz regime in 1911, Villa had enjoyed a peaceful interlude as a husband, father, and legitimate businessman. By the following year, however, plots against the government of his friend Madero caused him to strap on his guns again.

Francisco Madero was overwhelmingly elected president of Mexico in October 1911. He assumed office on November 6 and was hailed throughout Mexico as the "apostle of democracy." Unfortunately, the hope that Madero would be able to establish a viable government dedicated to moderate, gradual reform was quickly dashed. Former allies such as Orozco and Bernardo Reyes quickly betrayed him for personal gain and conspired with conservative elements led by Díaz's nephew, Felix Díaz, to foment rebellion.

Aware of what was going on around him, Madero summoned Villa to Mexico City and asked him to monitor Orozco's behavior. When Orozco declared his intention to overthrow the Madero government in February 1912, Villa quietly slipped out of the city with 11 followers and again headed into the mountains. Within a few days he was joined by 500 men, most of them former members of his old command.

For several weeks Villa conducted a single-handed campaign against Orozco's forces. After winning minor skirmishes at María del Oro and Guanacevi, he sent a clear message of warning to other garrisons contemplating treason: Villa ordered all of the prison-

ers—enlisted men as well as officers—executed. He
then managed to capture the important city of Parral,
but he did not have enough men or ammunition to
hold it. After a stubborn three-day defense against a
superior encircling force, he was forced to evacuate.

The situation deteriorated so rapidly in Mexico
that Madero was driven to appoint Victoriano Huerta,
a former general in the army of Díaz, to assume
command of all government troops. Huerta took control of the forces in northern Mexico, including those
of Villa and his men, on April 12, 1912. On May 23,
with Villa's irregular cavalry valiantly screening the
movements of Huerta's infantry, Huerta succeeded in
routing Orozco's army at the Battle of Tellano.

The relationship between Villa and Huerta had
been strained since the beginning: Villa was a proud
man who did not like to take orders from anyone, and
Huerta could not tolerate the least disobedience. But
what especially galled Villa was Huerta's condescending
attitude. With the Orozco threat removed, the dete-
rioration of the relationship was immediate and dramatic.

Despite, or perhaps because of, Villa's important
contribution to the defeat of Orozco, Huerta never
missed an opportunity to mock Villa's uncouth manners, limited education, and lack of proper military
attire. Villa stoically endured Huerta's sarcasm in si-
lence, but to salve his pride he decided to defy Huerta's
order against looting. He seized several magnificent
horses from a hacienda. As soon as Huerta found out,
he ordered Villa arrested.

At first Villa believed that his arrest was merely a
warning. But when he was sentenced to immediate
execution the next morning for insubordination, he
realized that his life was truly in jeopardy. Unable to
flee or obtain assistance from any of his followers, Villa
could only hope that President Madero would com-

Victoriano Huerta,
formerly a general
in Díaz's army, became
Villa's commander
in 1912. The two men
detested one another,
and when Villa defied an
order against looting,
Huerta had him arrested
and sentenced him
to death.

mute his sentence. Fortunately for Villa, Madero's brother Raul was traveling with the army and succeeded in getting in touch with the president by telegraph just in the nick of time. Villa was actually standing in front of the firing squad, waiting to hear the command to fire, when the cable announcing his reprieve was handed to the commanding officer. Much to Huerta's chagrin, he was ordered to transfer Villa to the military prison in Mexico City.

Upon Villa's arrival in Mexico City, President Madero commuted his sentence from death to two years in prison. Villa assumed, when he entered the minimum-security Santiago Tlatelolco prison, that he would be released in a few months. His accommodations were quite comfortable, befitting a hero of the Mexican Revolution. He was allowed to order his meals from an excellent restaurant and to hire a young tutor to visit him daily to help him improve his reading and writing. He studied his favorite book, *Napoléon's Campaigns,* for hours on end, fascinated by the strategy of the great 19th-century French general.

Six months later, in December, Villa was tired of waiting for the presidential pardon. He prevailed upon his tutor to bring him a sombrero, a shawl, and a pair of sunglasses. Then, disguised in these and other items of clothing he had accumulated, he took advantage of the lax security and simply walked out of the prison one day at the end of visiting hours. To avoid recapture in the nationwide search immediately launched, Villa relied upon tricks he had learned as a bandit. He took several taxi rides in false directions, traveled west by train instead of east to Veracruz, and then sailed by steamer from Mazatlán to Hermosillo. The final leg of his successful escape route was a dash across the border to Nogales, Arizona.

Villa walks away from a firing squad on the morning of October 26, 1912. The soldiers had their rifles raised and were awaiting the command to fire when a telegram arrived, announcing that President Madero had commuted the death sentence.

It is very likely that Villa's escape from prison and flight to the United States were aided by Madero loyalists. Several days before his prison break, he was visited by an agent of a group seeking his support for a plan to overthrow Madero. As soon as he arrived in Arizona, Villa communicated what he had learned about the plot to President Madero through Abrán González. González, now governor of Chihuahua, gave Villa 1,500 pesos and advised him to maintain a low profile.

Villa moved to El Paso, Texas. Using the name Jesús José Martínez, he registered at a small two-story hotel in the Mexican section of town, known as Little Chihuahua. Despite his attempt to remain incognito, in January 1913, Mexican and North American reporters announced his presence in the United States. Several even managed to obtain interviews with the reluctant fugitive.

During the two months he spent in El Paso, Villa became a frequent visitor to the Mexican Club, a cantina, café, dance hall, and casino that functioned as the social center of Little Chihuahua. Villa was constantly accompanied by several of his most loyal followers to protect him from assassination, but otherwise he lived quietly. He went out only at night and avoided contact with other revolutionary exiles in El Paso. To avoid any possibility of being arrested for engaging in revolutionary activity—a violation of U.S. neutrality laws—Villa kept in touch with his followers in Chihuahua via carrier pigeons.

The anti-Madero coup Villa had warned against began on February 9, 1913. Eight days after the fighting began, General Huerta betrayed Madero and seized control of the government. Both Madero and his vice-president were murdered by their military escort a few days later. There is little doubt that Huerta ordered their executions.

The murder of Madero unleashed a spasm of social upheaval in Mexico that kept the nation in political turmoil for the rest of the decade. Huerta's authority to rule was almost immediately challenged by a number of rivals, the most notable of whom were Villa, Zapata, and Venustiano Carranza, the governor of the state of Cohahuila. Madero's name became a symbol of revolutionary unity in the continuing struggle against military despotism—now represented by the Huerta regime.

Carranza promised to continue the reforms Madero had begun and declared himself the head of the Constitutionalist movement. Villa, dedicated to avenging the death of his friend Madero and eliminating the detested Huerta, borrowed money to purchase supplies and set out for Chihuahua City with eight followers.

Unable to secure horses legally because of U.S. neutrality laws and the vigilance of Huerta agents in El Paso, Villa employed a simple but effective trick. For more than a week, he and his men rented horses from a livery stable for an evening ride. Sometimes they did not return the mounts until very late. When they did not return at all one night, the stable owner assumed that they would bring the mounts back in the morning and went to bed. He was wrong. Under cover of darkness, Villa and his eight companions galloped across the Rio Grande into Mexico.

Villa's assumption that his followers would rally to his side as soon as he returned to Chihuahua proved correct. Within a month his army of eight had grown to over 500 men.

While Villa was gathering his forces, Carranza's military commander, Alvaro Obregón, captured the border town of Nogales in Sonora. Obregón's humble origins mirrored Villa's, but he had never become a bandit. Although he did not participate in the over-

Torreón, Mexico, as it appeared in 1913, when Villa made it the focus of his campaign against the Huerta government. In order to capture the important rail junction, Villa launched a series of assaults on surrounding towns, slowly tightening the noose on his ultimate objective.

throw of Díaz in the 1910–11 rebellion, his commitment to implementing the social reforms of the revolution never wavered. Largely self-educated, he proved to be the most willing of all the Mexican citizen-generals to learn modern military strategy and fighting techniques. Still, Villa's charismatic leadership and ability to recruit thousands of men enabled him to completely overshadow Obregón in 1912.

Carranza and Villa were united only by their common opposition to Huerta. After his bitter experience serving under Huerta, Villa was not about to recognize any superior military chain of command. When emissaries of Carranza met with Villa in Asunción, Villa made it clear that he was a caudillo—a general in charge of his own army who took orders from no one. Carranza gracefully accepted Villa's terms and recognized the obvious by appointing him commander of all Constitutionalist forces in Chihuahua. In return, Villa agreed to recognize Carranza as first chief of the Constitutionalist revolutionary government. Villa gave himself the title commander in chief of the Division of the North.

Villa spent most of the summer of 1913 secretly obtaining military supplies for his growing army. It was illegal for North Americans to sell military equipment and ammunition in Mexico, but smugglers were willing to provide virtually anything Villa wanted as long as he paid their exorbitant prices in gold. In this manner, Villa soon had his forces ready for battle.

On August 25, 1913, at the head of 1,200 cavalry, Villa attacked San Andrés, a town west of Chihuahua City. He overwhelmed the federal garrison of 2,000 and seized half a dozen railway trains crammed with military supplies and ammunition. With this bonanza, he was able to equip the hundreds of recruits that were streaming into his camp every day.

Villa's forces storm a government position in November 1913. Villa had previously limited himself to the hit-and-run tactics he had employed as a bandit; at Torreón and Tierra Blanca, he proved himself equally skilled at commanding masses of troops in a formal battle.

Villa had carefully planned his campaign while in exile in Texas. His next target was the vital rail junction of Torreón. The battle for the city began on September 29, 1913. In the course of the next two days, often in hand-to-hand combat, Villa's men attacked the surrounding towns of La Loma, Alvarez, Aviles, and Lerdo, forcing the government defenders to fall back into Torreón's defensive perimeter.

On the evening of the third day, Villa's forces took Torreón in a mass assault led by Yaqui Indian warriors. On October 1, Villa formally occupied the city. He celebrated the occasion by personally shooting 50 captured federal officers. The next day he ordered all Spanish citizens living within the city to abandon their personal property and leave the city within three hours. Failure to comply warranted immediate execution.

The victory at Torreón proved that Villa was capable of leading a large army to victory in a formal battle. The techniques he had developed as a young man living on the run in the mountains of Chihuahua had proved invaluable to his earlier success as a guerrilla fighter. Now he showed what he had learned from his study of Napoléon's campaigns while in prison. General Francisco Villa was no longer an impulsive guerrilla unit leader, but an administrator, strategist, and organizer in charge of some 10,000 troops. The vast amounts of military equipment he obtained— cannons, rifles, ammunition, an armored railway car, 40 locomotives, and several whole trains—made his army superior to any other revolutionary force in Mexico. The fugitive had become the hunter, the bandit a rebel general bent on revenge.

DICTATOR
OF THE NORTH

Fittingly attired in a formal military uniform, Villa found himself in 1913 the most powerful general in Mexico. As commander of the Army of the North and virtual dictator of Chihuahua, he gained international renown—U.S. officials believed that he was certain to become president of Mexico.

The power that Villa's army and battle successes conferred upon him drew him to the attention of American and European world leaders in 1913. For the first time, his behavior after a battle was held up to international examination. His continuation of the Mexican custom of executing all captured enemy officers attracted almost as much hostile criticism as his maltreatment of Spanish citizens. Many of the Spanish women and children he expelled from Torreón died trying to make their way across the desert; Villa had forbidden them to use the railroad.

Like many of his compatriots, Villa believed that all Spaniards were supporters of Huerta. There was a great deal of popular prejudice against Spaniards within the Mexican population. Most Mexicans were mestizos, people of mixed Spanish and Indian heritage, and they were well aware that pure-blooded Spaniards looked down upon them. The Spanish had conquered the ancient Indian civilizations of Mexico during the 16th century, and nearly 400 years later, they served as the managers of the institutions that weighed most heavily on the common people: banks, haciendas, and mining companies.

After expelling the Spanish, Villa held 50 German, English, French, and Italian citizens as hostages to prevent a government counterattack. No restrictions were placed on the movement of North Americans, for Villa was much too shrewd to provide any provocation for U.S. military intervention. When he caught several of his men disregarding his orders to loot only Spanish property, he shot them on the spot. Many more of his men were executed by firing squads for drinking to excess and molesting innocent civilians. The message got through: Villa's troops were extremely well behaved for such a mixed force of volunteers.

Villa's next target after Torreón was Chihuahua City, which he captured on December 8, after a strategic retreat, a daring raid on Ciudad Juárez, and a smashing victory at Tierra Blanca.

Villa's vicious prejudice against Spaniards surfaced again in Chihuahua. The 400 Spanish residents of the city were given five days to leave or face execution. Villa claimed that he had to expel all Spanish citizens into the desert in order to save them from being massacred. Still, compared to his treatment of any wealthy hacienda owners who fell into his hands, his behavior toward the Spanish community was quite humane.

The audacity, ingenuity, and efficiency of Villa's campaign seized the imagination of North Americans as well as Mexicans. Headlines trumpeting his victories blazed across newspapers in the United States. Businessmen with investments in Mexico appreciated the need to be on the winning side. New recruits and funds to acquire military supplies in the United States suddenly became available.

During the year that Villa occupied Juárez, he paved its streets, rebuilt its hospitals, developed its railroads, built new schools, raised teachers' salaries, cooperated with American narcotics officers to stop the flow of drugs across the border, and carefully collected import and export duties. Unfortunately, he also imposed exorbitant taxes, seized private property at will without providing compensation, crushed labor unrest, allowed gambling and prostitution, and ruled by decree. In effect, he preached democracy but practiced despotism.

By January 1, 1914, Villa was, for all practical purposes, the military dictator of the state of Chihuahua. He appointed a full complement of his own men (chosen for loyalty, not competence) to fill all levels of government offices. His influence, if not his direct control, extended over most of northern Mexico. All the industrial, labor, and tax revenue–generating sources he could grasp were marshaled to support his burgeoning war machine.

A firing squad executes a trio of prisoners in northern Mexico. As Villa achieved world fame, his methods also came under closer scrutiny. Though he was praised for improving living conditions in Chihuahua, his practice of routinely shooting captured officers and mistreating Europeans drew strong criticism.

Villa's fame far surpassed that of his nominal superior, Venustiano Carranza. To European leaders and U.S. president Woodrow Wilson, Villa was no longer one of the countless generals south of the Rio Grande but someone who had to be dealt with when deciding major U.S. policies in Mexico. Villa, acutely aware of the new status he had acquired, demonstrated considerable political savvy. He cultivated the favor of the international press by granting interviews and was careful to treat foreign diplomats with patience and tact. He even authorized the production of silent movies to be shown in the United States about his exploits. His efforts paid off. The prestigious *New York Times,* in an article about his life, referred to Villa as the Robin Hood of Mexico. On February 3, 1914, President Wilson, eager to encourage Huerta's overthrow, lifted the embargo prohibiting American merchants from selling military equipment to Mexican insurgents.

Villa's prestige was so high in early 1914 that most U.S. officials were convinced that once Huerta was eliminated, Villa would succeed him. President Wilson dispatched U.S. officials to Mexico to assess the situation. Despite Villa's lack of commitment to any specific program of reform—other than a vague wish to take from the rich and give to the poor—the reports Wilson received encouraged him to believe that Villa might be the right individual to restore order in Mexico while continuing the reforms begun by Madero. In the turmoil of Mexico's civil war, Villa's persecution of Spanish citizens was overshadowed by his military successes and the failings of Huerta.

Villa learned the limits of his foreign popularity during the so-called Benton affair. William S. Benton, a British citizen, owned a large hacienda in Chihuahua. Angered by the continued confiscation of his cattle by Villa's men, Benton barged into Villa's headquarters one day in late February and voiced his complaint. Benton and Villa engaged in a violent quarrel. Apparently Benton believed that, as in previous disputes with Villa, his British citizenship would protect him. He was wrong. Villa arrested him. After a speedy trial, Benton was convicted and shot.

Benton's fate was no different from that of any Mexican who dared to challenge Villa's authority, but the international press and diplomatic community reacted with outrage. Villa was genuinely shocked that one foreigner's death could cost him so much of the goodwill he had gained abroad. He learned, in essence, that he could get away with murder as long as he did not kill the wrong people. He was careful not to repeat the same mistake.

During his highly successful 1914 spring military campaign, Villa showed that he had learned his lesson well. He ordered his sophisticated medical unit to care for wounded prisoners, and he gave captured officers a trial before shooting them. He also told U.S. consul Theodore C. Hamm that, in view of the fact that the United States had lifted its embargo against his obtaining military supplies, he would not require North Americans shipping merchandise out of northern Mexico to pay any export taxes. Before long, he had a chance to play an even bigger role in U.S.-Mexican relations.

On April 22, 1914, U.S. Marines landed in the port city of Veracruz to punish the Huerta regime for harassing a group of U.S. naval personnel. The marines arrived as a German freighter, the *Ypiranga,* was about to unload a cargo of ammunition for the federal army. When the marines tried to prevent the delivery, cadets from the Mexican Naval Institute opened fire on them. In the two-day battle that followed, the marines succeeded in crushing all armed Mexican resistance within the city.

The invasion of Veracruz aroused a wave of popular indignation throughout Mexico. Once again, the bully of the North had impinged upon Mexican territorial sovereignty. Huerta attempted to take advantage of the popular furor. He invited Carranza, Villa, and Zapata to join him in a national coalition to drive the Yankees out. They refused.

Carranza attempted to follow a moderate course. Although he was personally angered by the American incursion, he was also a realist. He wrote and published a fierce letter of protest to President Wilson, primarily for domestic consumption; but he did not accept General Obregón's advice to fight, mainly because he knew that he could not count on the support of Villa.

The USS Michigan *(center) and other warships occupy the harbor of Veracruz, Mexico, in April 1914, seeking to avenge a number of insults from the Huerta government. In the United States, the occupation was hailed as a defense of national honor; Mexicans condemned it as the act of a bully.*

For several months in 1914, the situation in Mexico was extremely delicate. Mexico and the United States were on the brink of war. If Villa had agreed to join forces with Huerta, a war the United States did not want and Mexico could not afford probably would have started. But Villa was not about to fall into an alliance with Huerta for any reason, especially not to fight the country from which he was obtaining all his military supplies.

The United States found itself in the awkward position of occupying a Mexican city in the midst of a civil war, without the support of either the regime in power or the opposition. To help resolve the impasse, the United States encouraged Argentina, Brazil, and Chile to offer their services as mediators. President Wilson hoped that Latin American diplomats might be able to find some way to combine the evacuation of Veracruz, the resignation of Huerta, and the establishment of a constitutional regime in Mexico. The so-called ABC conference, held in May at Niagara Falls, Canada, accomplished nothing specific, but it did provide an opportunity for Carranza to seize the international diplomatic spotlight. Without consulting Villa, he dispatched three delegates to represent the Constitutionalist movement.

When Villa protested that Carranza should have discussed the matter with him, Carranza telegraphed each of the Army of the North's generals and asked them for their support. He also asked them to swear their loyalty to the Constitutionalist cause rather than to any one man. General Felipe Angeles, Villa's second-in-command, framed the response of Villa's officers to Carranza's telegram. It was a firm statement of loyalty to Villa.

On June 15, Villa replied to Carranza's effort to undermine his authority by formally resigning as commander in chief of the Army of the North. He further announced that, from that day forward, he would operate independently for the pacification of Mexico and the establishment of constitutional government and economic reform.

Fortunately, both men realized that the only beneficiary of a clash between them would be their mutual enemy Huerta. Common sense prevailed, and Villa and Carranza were able to negotiate an agreement on July 9 at Torreón, which temporarily prevented a complete rupture. The agreement provided for a convention to be held in Mexico City, as soon as Huerta had been overthrown, for the purpose of writing a constitution and creating a provisional government.

Delegates to the ABC Conference gather in front of the Prospect Hotel in Niagara Falls, Canada, in May 1914. The conference did not directly settle the dispute between the United States and Mexico, but it paved the way for the resignation of Huerta and the adoption of reforms in Mexico.

Convention delegates, 1 for every 1,000 soldiers in each revolutionary army, were to be elected by committees of senior officers, subject to approval by the respective division commanders. Civil government was to be reestablished as soon as possible through open national elections. Military leaders were specifically prohibited from holding the office of president or governor.

Despite the apparent reconciliation, there was no longer any trust or respect between Carranza and Villa. Publicly, Carranza ignored Villa's declaration of independence and ordered him, much to Villa's amusement, to proceed with the military campaign to overthrow Huerta. However, behind the scenes, Carranza began the process of undermining Villa's power by disrupting his supplies of coal and ammunition. Without coal to fuel his steam locomotives, Villa's trains could not move. Villa suspected that Carranza was behind the supply shortages, but he had no evidence and little choice but to overlook the matter until he had eliminated Huerta.

Once he was sure that there would be no war between Mexico and the United States, Villa resumed his march south. On June 23, his army captured Zacatecas, the last Huerta stronghold. On July 15, 1914, Huerta resigned and fled the country.

The celebration over Huerta's demise was short-lived. The tension between Villa and Carranza, contained during the assault on their mutual enemy, now flared openly. Carranza immediately moved to seize the reins of power by establishing his provisional government in office and declaring himself president. Villa, convinced of Carranza's treachery, increased his recruitment efforts and withdrew his army to the north.

The root of the problem between Villa and Carranza was simple: each believed that the other had no

Venustiano Carranza, photographed in 1915, after he had succeeded Huerta as president of Mexico. Carranza and Villa had clashed repeatedly when both were rebel generals, and the new president believed that he could not govern Mexico unless he brought Villa under control.

intention of implementing reform and only wanted to become a dictator. Both were, in their own way, quite appealing revolutionary leaders. A U.S. diplomat who met Villa at this time described him as an "unusually quiet man, gentle in manner, low voiced, slow of speech, earnest, and occasionally emotional in expression, but always subdued, with an undercurrent of sadness." Another diplomat described Carranza as "a man of force and no mean ability. One of Mexico's ablest officials, and a man of strict integrity." The tragedy was that there was not enough room in Mexico's turbulent revolutionary political arena for both men to prevail, and they knew it.

MASTER OF MEXICO

Villa and his wife, María Luz, stroll through the streets of Juárez in 1914. Though he faithfully provided for his family, Villa was a man of ungovernable passions, and his pursuit of women sometimes caused embarrassing scandals.

On August 15, 1914, General Alvaro Obregón's forces occupied Mexico City. Five days later Carranza triumphantly entered the city and assumed control of the government. Neither Villa nor any of his troops participated in the victory celebrations.

The first actual fighting between Carranza's and Villa's troops occurred at Naco, in the state of Sonora. Because Naco straddled the U.S. border, shots fired in the Mexican section wounded several U.S. citizens. This incident, plus the concern of U.S. diplomats that the fighting would spread throughout Mexico, prompted a U.S. mediation attempt. President Wilson desperately wanted peace in Mexico and a stable democratic government.

In late August, discussions between Obregón and Villa were mediated by U.S. representatives. Villa set the congenial tone of the negotiations when he greeted Obregón with the comment: "Look here, my friend—if you had come with troops, we would have received you with bullets, but since you come alone, you are perfectly safe; Francisco Villa is not treacherous. The destinies of our country are in your hands and mine."

Under the terms of the agreement hammered out between Villa and Obregón, Villa ordered his troops to give up their attempt to capture Naco. In return, Obregón promised that the Constitutionalist troops would not use the town as a base for attacking Villa's men. The two men parted company at the conclusion of the negotiations with what appeared to be a strong bond of friendship. The threat of renewed civil war in Mexico appeared to have been avoided. Villa once again recognized Carranza as his nominal superior.

On September 15, 1914, President Wilson finally ordered the withdrawal of U.S. forces from Veracruz. The stage appeared set for peace in Mexico, except for two problems: Villa, not Carranza, still controlled the most powerful army in Mexico; and Emiliano Zapata, who had been in rebellion since the first days of the revolt against Díaz, trusted Villa more than Carranza.

Most Mexican and foreign observers assumed that it would only be a matter of time until the rift between Villa and Carranza opened again, but they were surprised by the swiftness of the explosion. When Obregón returned to continue negotiations with Villa in Chihuahua, he and Villa quarreled over the exact terms of the Naco truce agreement. Villa believed that Obregón was obliged to order the withdrawal of the Constitutionalist garrison in Naco now that Villa's troops had been moved to the south. Obregón disagreed. In the absence of U.S. mediators, the discussion quickly degenerated into a shouting match. Villa became so enraged that he ordered his men to surround the building they were meeting in. Then he informed the ashen-faced Obregón that he and his aide were about to be executed.

Even in the face of death, Obregón refused to back down. Fortunately, some of the calmer members of Villa's staff persuaded their chief to relent. Instead of carrying out his deadly threat, Villa broke off the

Alvaro Obregón (center), photographed in 1913, when he was a colonel in the Constitutionalist army. As a general representing the Carranza government, Obregón negotiated with Villa in late 1914; at first he made progress, but when Villa finally lost his temper, Obregón had to flee for his life.

discussions and authorized Obregón and his aide to return by train to Mexico City. He evidently changed his mind soon after Obregón had begun his journey, because a telegraph message was sent to stop Obregón's train at Torreón and to take him prisoner. However, Obregón knew enough about Villa to understand why his train was being held up, and he made his escape before Villa's men could capture him.

Villa's treatment of Obregón prompted Carranza to halt all railway traffic north of Aguascalientes. He also ordered Constitutionalist forces to prevent Villa's troops from moving south. Villa responded by declaring on September 22 that he no longer recognized Carranza as a leader of the revolution, because he had not implemented any of the reforms they had agreed to at their conference in July at Torreón.

There was one slender hope of avoiding a new civil war in Mexico. In their Torreón discussions, Villa and Carranza had agreed to a national convention in Mexico City. Here, representatives of all the revolutionary factions would hammer out the details for the establishment of a new government.

The convention first met in Mexico City at the end of September. Because the capital was Carranza's home ground, Villa and Zapata felt that he would control the convention, and both stayed away. To appease them, the delegates voted on October 5 to adjourn the meeting and reconvene it 10 days later in Aguascalientes. Their strategy worked, and Villa and Zapata decided to participate after all. Villa addressed the assembled delegates and, in a moving speech, promised that neither he nor any of his generals would ever be candidates for the presidency or the governorship of any state. He promised to support anyone but Carranza as provisional president. Zapata backed Villa's position on Carranza. On November 2, the two rebel leaders secured the choice of a compromise candidate, General Eulalio Gutiérrez. Carranza was ordered to leave office on November 10.

Carranza immediately denounced the decision, claiming that the delegates were intimidated by the large number of Villista troops in and around Aguascalientes. Instead of surrendering his office to Gutiérrez, he ordered his generals to return to their commands in order to prepare for battle. A vicious new phase of the Mexican Revolution had begun.

On November 19, 1914, after a formal declaration of war by Obregón, Villa began moving his formidable army south. He had 40,000 fully equipped men, a reserve supply of 240 carloads of coal, from 250 to 300 carloads of provisions, and an ample number of railroad cars and locomotives.

Carranza realized that he had no military force capable of stopping Villa. He wisely accepted General Obregón's advice to abandon the capital and retreat to Veracruz. With Carranza's military forces in retreat, Villa's march south turned from a military campaign into a victory procession. As opposed to his earlier campaigns, Villa now took the time to replace the local government officials with his own men. He meant to establish permanent political control to match his military domination.

On December 2, 1914, Villa announced that he would wait for Zapata to join him before entering Mexico City, so that they could share the glory together. Four days later, Villa, dressed in an elaborate dark blue suit trimmed with gold, joined Zapata, who

General Emiliano Zapata (seated at center) with members of his staff in 1912. Zapata was as powerful in southern Mexico as Villa was in the north; both of peasant stock, the rebel generals shared a mutual admiration and a deep distrust of middle-class politicians such as Huerta and Carranza.

was wearing a peasant outfit and a wide sombrero. The two men, riding side by side, led a 30,000-man victory parade through the streets of the capital.

Zapata was the most steadfast opponent of all of the regimes that followed Díaz. With a strong base of support in his native state of Morelos, he had repeatedly called his countrymen to arms. Like Villa, he had witnessed the steady contraction of village lands during the Díaz regime and viewed this injustice as the root of Mexico's social ills. Because Madero, Huerta, and Carranza all failed to give land back to the peasants quickly enough to suit Zapata, he eventually opposed each of them by force.

Contrary to fears fanned by Carranza, the Villista and Zapatista troops did not loot or execute thousands of citizens. The commanders maintained public order and firmly enforced military discipline. The executions that did take place occurred discreetly in the middle of the night—so discreetly, in fact, that there is no way to determine exactly how many there were or how much direct responsibility Villa should bear. Offsetting the grisly tales of midnight executions were reports that Villa rounded up most of the war orphans from the streets of Mexico City and sent them to Chihuahua to be cared for and educated at his expense.

Villa remained in the capital long enough to embroil himself in an affair that did nothing to boost his image. He often dined at an elegant hotel, and a young Frenchwoman who worked there as a cashier made the mistake of flirting with him. Villa did not take such matters lightly. He immediately proposed marriage; when the woman failed to respond, he carried her off to his private residence and summoned a priest to perform a bogus wedding ceremony. Fortunately for Villa's unwilling bride, the priest was slow in arriving. Meanwhile, the French ambassador was alerted and warned Villa that his actions could lead to a serious international incident. Remembering the Benson affair and finding the young woman violently opposed to his advances, Villa decided to take the advice of his aides and let his captive go. Even so, the incident made the newspapers around the world and was used as propaganda against the revolution.

Although Gutiérrez was Mexico's provisional president, Villa and Zapata, the real centers of power, paid attention to his directives only when it was convenient. The situation finally became so intolerable for Gutiérrez that, after being in office for only two months, he resigned and fled into exile. The convention immediately named another man, González Garza, to take Gutiérrez's place, but he too quickly realized that he was just a figurehead.

In January 1915, Villa decided to begin the campaign to drive Carranza out of Veracruz by capturing Tampico and seizing the Coahuila coalfields. Controlling the capital was impressive, but until Obregón was defeated and Carranza eliminated, there would be no peace in Mexico. On February 4, 1915, Villa withdrew from Mexico City and returned to his headquarters in Chihuahua, where he established a provisional government and named himself president. He was now openly aiming to be the military dictator of Mexico.

Villa did not care about the loss of the capital; he was sure he could reoccupy it as soon as he eliminated Obregón's army. To offset Villa's huge numerical advantage, Obregón shrewdly moved his men into defensive positions near the town of Celaya, about 150 miles northwest of Mexico City.

Obregón had been following the battles of World War I, which had broken out in Europe in August 1914. He fully appreciated the advantages that deep trenches, massed artillery, and machine guns could provide an army. He chose to make his stand at Celaya

because it was surrounded by an intricate network of irrigation ditches. Obregón ordered the ditches drained, reinforced, and laced with barbed wire. Then he positioned his troops and awaited Villa's onslaught.

After surveying reports of Obregón's fortifications, Felipe Angeles counseled Villa to avoid falling into a trap. It would be far better, he and other officers argued, to fight Obregón on more suitable terrain. Villa, flushed with his string of military victories, arrogantly ignored this advice. On April 6, he launched a massive frontal assault against Obregón's trenches. For more than a week, in a replay of the slaughter taking place in the trenches of France, wave after wave of Villa's infantry and cavalry were cut to pieces by Obregón's machine guns and field artillery. Villa's hospital train was overwhelmed on the first day of battle with more than 1,000 casualties. The second day of the battle led to the same dismal results, but with twice as many casualties.

Villa gallops alongside his army as he takes the offensive against the Carranza government in 1914. At the height of his power, Villa planned to smash the pro-Carranza forces commanded by Obregón and then take command of Mexico City.

The loss of 3,000 men in two days forced Villa to withdraw. Angeles, not at the battle site because of a successful effort by one of Obregón's divisions to delay his column's advance, pleaded with Villa to wait until he could join him before launching any more assaults, but the arrival of 5,000 reinforcements provided too much temptation. Villa decided to return for another attack.

At dawn on April 13, vast clouds of dust alerted Obregón that Villa's army was about to begin a second offensive. Obregón was ready. He had taken advantage of the lull in the fighting to further improve his fortifications. New mines, additional barbed wire, and machine-gun bunkers awaited Villa's men. Villa's first tactic was to repeat the approach that had already failed: he ordered massive infantry and cavalry assaults all along Obregón's perimeter. The bodies of men and horses piled so high in front of the machine-gun bunkers that later waves of attackers used them for cover until they too were killed.

Desperate, with half his reinforcements already virtually wiped out, Villa decided to concentrate all his men for a charge upon one spot in the perimeter. He was convinced that the sheer weight of their assault would enable his brave men to carry the day. He was wrong. Obregón, well prepared for just such a tactic, ordered all his artillery focused on the exposed mass of men. The concentration of large numbers of men in one spot is suicidal in modern warfare, and the carnage at Celaya was horrific. Thousands of Villa's men were blown to bits long before they even reached the first line of defense. The attack turned into a retreat, and the retreat turned into a rout. Obregón's cavalry completed the massacre: they pounced upon the beaten men in a mad frenzy of slashing sabers.

The next morning, Villa, aware that he had lost half of his once proud army because of his mistakes in judgment and poor strategic planning, accepted defeat. Despite his immense casualties, he was still able to execute an orderly withdrawal from Celaya.

The defeat at Celaya was the decisive turning point of Villa's military career. The qualities that had led him to success up to that time—courage, refusal to accept defeat, audacity, personal leadership—were the characteristics that Obregón was able to turn to his own advantage. After Celaya, the offensive momentum shifted to Obregón.

Although Villa's army had been badly mauled, it had not been destroyed. It still constituted a force of more than 10,000 men. Both Villa and Obregón knew

Obregón's troops inspect rifles captured from Villa's soldiers in 1915. By employing the most advanced military tactics, Obregón gained decisive victories at Celaya and Aguascalientes and effectively destroyed Villa's chances of ruling Mexico.

that at least one more major battle would have to be fought to determine whose army would prevail. Villa prepared for the battle by concentrating his forces in the vicinity of Aguascalientes, obtaining reinforcements by halting operations against Tampico and withdrawing troops from other areas such as Monterrey and Matamoros.

Villa was finally ready to listen to Felipe Angeles, but it was too late. Early in June, near the city of León, in a series of pitched battles, Obregón's brilliant grasp of modern tactics enabled him to defeat Villa's forces soundly. Obregón had his right arm blown off at the elbow by an artillery barrage early in the fighting, but he survived surgery and remained in command.

Although Villa's army was able to retreat north from León in good order to Durango, two major defeats in close succession destroyed his reputation as an invincible military leader. Desertions increased rapidly. While his army dwindled, Obregón's grew.

Villa maintained control of northern Mexico during the summer of 1915, but he was unable to prevent Obregón from defeating Zapata's forces and occupying Mexico City. By the fall of 1915, the situation was far from settled in Mexico, but with Obregón's victories, the balance of power shifted heavily back to Carranza.

THE
TURNING TIDE

A confident-looking Villa visits his troops during the campaign against Carranza. Despite his defeats at Celaya and Aguascalientes, Villa was still convinced that he could overthrow the government—however, he recognized that he would need aid from the United States and tried to cultivate goodwill north of the border.

When Woodrow Wilson became president of the United States in March 1913, he was so appalled by the murder of President Madero by General Huerta that he refused to recognize Huerta's regime. The desire to encourage Huerta's demise also lay behind Wilson's decision to lift the U.S. embargo against supplying military equipment to Mexicans.

After Huerta's downfall, Wilson adopted a policy of "watchful waiting," undecided whether to support Villa or Carranza. Both sides recognized the huge impact American support would have, but Villa responded more promptly to diplomatic requests than Carranza, and this helped him cultivate favorable U.S. opinion.

Unfortunately for Villa, his bandit past, casual disregard for human life, numerous wives and lovers, and reliance upon military power to achieve political ends provided his enemies with plenty of ammunition. They used it to keep up a steady stream of hostile propaganda about Villa in both Mexico and the United States and undermined his efforts to portray himself as a dedicated revolutionary leader.

The standoff that had been negotiated between Villa and Carranza forces involving the border community of Naco, Sonora, broke down in the fall of 1915. Once again the United States became directly involved because the fighting between the Mexican factions was spilling over the border. When U.S. protests produced no results, President Wilson ordered General Hugh L. Scott to cable Villa in Chihuahua City and warn him that unless the fighting stopped U.S. troops would intervene.

When he arrived in Naco in October 1915, Villa found that his ally Governor José María Maytorena had entrenched his forces in front of the defenses of General Plutarco Calles. Villa, against Maytorena's protests, stopped the siege and ordered the troops back to

Villa and General Hugh L. Scott of the U.S. Army emerge from their 1915 conference. According to Scott, the two men were "locked for two hours like bulls with their horns crossed," but in the end Villa agreed to Scott's demand that his forces end their hostilities along the U.S. border.

Hermosillo. Calles withdrew his men to Agua Prieta. An agreement was made that Naco would remain neutral territory. Neither side really planned to abide by the agreement, but the mutual pullback satisfied the U.S. government.

Despite Villa's cooperation, Wilson was convinced by the fall of 1915 that Carranza had a better chance than Villa of establishing a stable government that could improve the lives of the masses of Mexicans. On October 15, 1915, the United States formally recognized the Carranza regime as the government of Mexico. The impact upon Villa was immediate: Wilson prohibited the sale of military equipment and supplies destined for Villa, but he authorized such sales to the Carranza government. As far as the United States was concerned, Villa was no longer a revolutionary; he was now an outlaw and the leader of a gang of bandits.

News of Wilson's decision reached Villa in Chihuahua while he was busy reorganizing his much-diminished but still formidable army. He undoubtedly felt betrayed, but he made no public statement. Recent casualties and desertions had considerably reduced the number of troops under his command, but he was not beaten yet. A major victory could reverse his precipitous decline.

Agua Prieta, opposite the U.S. city of Douglas, Arizona, was the logical place for Villa to attack. Its garrison was the only Carranza force in northern Sonora. By capturing Agua Prieta, Villa could eliminate an enemy threat to his rear and obtain another border entry point for obtaining smuggled military supplies from the United States.

Villa's ability to attack the isolated garrison with the entire weight of his reorganized 10,000-man army appeared to assure victory. The problem was that both the Carranza and U.S. governments also realized that Agua Prieta presented an ideal target. This time Villa would not have the element of surprise in his favor. When his army disappeared from sight in order to conduct its long march to the northwest in secrecy, President Wilson allowed Obregón to reinforce Agua Prieta by transporting troops from Piedras Negras on the Texas-Coahuila border, a distance of 600 miles through U. S. territory, over U.S. railway lines.

By the time Villa's army reached Agua Prieta, the town had been converted into an almost impregnable fortress. Trainloads of troops, artillery, munitions, and equipment had arrived, and General Plutarco Calles had surrounded the town on three sides with deep trenches, mountains of barbed wire, powerful spot-lights, and hundreds of machine guns. The fourth side faced U.S. territory, so it needed no defenses.

Villa learned of the U.S. decision to formally recognize and aid the Carranza government when he arrived at the outskirts of Agua Prieta. He was enraged by the new U.S. policy. Ever since the overthrow of Díaz, the United States had been careful not to give any material aid to any faction in Mexico. No armed Mexican forces had ever been permitted on U.S. soil. Now, suddenly, the rules had been changed. The Car-ranza forces had unlimited access to military equip-ment; Villa had none. The Carranza forces could travel through U.S. territory; Villa's men could not. Villa vowed that he would capture Agua Prieta anyway.

The three-day battle began on November 1, 1915, with an artillery duel. Villa decided to use the rest of the day to probe the town's defenses with three cav-alry charges. As the first wave of Villa's horsemen charged across the open plain, a cold wind off the desert whipped up a great cloud of dust that partially concealed the attackers from enemy fire. Nevertheless, artillery and machine-gun fire forced them to pull back to the town's outskirts. Two more charges on the other sides of the city's defensive perimeter produced

Woodrow Wilson, president of the United States from 1912 to 1920, decided in the fall of 1915 that the Carranza regime represented the best hope of stability in Mexico. Villa was dismayed and angered by Wilson's decision, which made it impossible for Villa to obtain weapons and supplies from U.S. firms.

the same disheartening results. The small number who did manage to reach the town were quickly mowed down by enemy cross fire.

Villa's generals counseled withdrawal, but Villa was not ready to countenance retreat. He sought to overcome Calles's defensive advantage by launching his main assault under the cover of darkness. Prior to the 1:30 A.M. signal to attack, Villa's Yaqui Indian troops silently crept through a line of barbed wire, preparing to throw hand grenades into the enemy fortifications. It was a sound plan, but the element of surprise was missing because Calles had anticipated the strategy and prepared a surprise of his own. As the Yaquis began their assault, Calles's men switched on huge electric searchlights, turning night into day. The Yaquis were trapped. They could not advance into the blinding light, and the barbed wire was at their backs. They could only stay where they were and be slaughtered. The comrades who rushed forward to help them suffered the same fate.

The full magnitude of the catastrophe did not become apparent until the next morning, when thousands of corpses could be seen covering the battlefield. The combination of the searchlights and machine guns added a new element to the struggle between Villa and Carranza. There was no doubt in Villa's mind that the lights, and the electricity and expertise necessary to operate them, had been provided by the United States.

Villa's previous victories had brought recruits flocking to his banner; his defeats caused his forces to wither away. To make it easier for his men to gather food during their retreat south, he divided the remnants of his army into three groups. Each group was ordered to forage along a different path until it reached Hermosillo, where the army would reunite. But only the group personally commanded by Villa arrived in

Hermosillo. The other two groups simply disbanded along the way.

Villa expressed his resentment against the United States by demanding that every U.S. mining company in his area give him a loan of $25,000 or be confiscated. He and his men now regarded any U.S. property they could get their hands on as theirs for the taking.

Villa realized that he was running out of time. The longer he waited, the more strength his enemies derived from U.S. aid. He knew that his battered army was still capable of one more major offensive, and he decided to attack Hermosillo. Because he no longer had the funds to pay his men, Villa promised that they would be free to loot the city.

The battle for Hermosillo in mid-November 1915 was a less dramatic but even more shattering defeat for Villa than Agua Prieta. Once again the discipline and bravery of Villa's troops gave way before artillery barrages and the withering cross fire of machine guns. They were not even allowed the dignity of an orderly retreat; now equipped with long-range artillery, Carranza's men kept firing at Villa's forces, turning their withdrawal into a panic-stricken rout. The carnage that U.S. aid enabled Carranza forces to inflict at Agua Prieta and Hermosillo effectively destroyed Villa's army. He could never again mount a significant military threat to the Carranza government.

As the remnants of Villa's disintegrating army gradually drifted northward toward Nogales in unruly packs, they committed numerous atrocities. Villa was powerless to control his men. He may even have encouraged them. Witnesses testified that because ammunition was low, he killed prisoners by lining them up one behind the other, placing a rife against the chest of the first man, and firing. He would then determine how many had died, roll them out of the way, line up the survivors, and repeat the process.

When Villa's soldiers reached the border community of Nogales, their rage at the United States for interfering in Mexican affairs could not be contained. On November 25, several soldiers, brandishing their weapons, rode across the international boundary to threaten two U.S. officials. Anticipating more trouble, the regional U.S. military commander quickly beefed up the local garrison with reinforcements and authorized his troops to return any hostile fire. Gunfire from the Mexican side of the border provoked several intense firefights before the pursuing Carranza forces finally occupied Nogales on November 26.

Mexican president Carranza poses with new recruits to his army in 1915. Bolstered by new equipment from the United States, including the latest machine guns, Carranza's forces inflicted two more crushing defeats on Villa at Agua Prieta and Hermosillo.

The same pattern of hostile behavior and shooting across the border was repeated in Ciudad Juárez until Carranza forces took possession of that city on December 23, 1915. With the capture of Juárez, the defeat of Villa in northern Mexico seemed so complete that U.S. diplomats confidently predicted his imminent flight to the United States.

Instead of seeking political asylum across the border, Villa returned to Chihuahua City. There, in a stormy meeting, his generals informed him that he could no longer count on their loyalty. The new U.S. policy of supporting Carranza seemed to have accomplished its objective. Villa appeared finished as a serious threat to the stability of the government. With a small band of his most loyal followers, Villa disappeared into the rugged Sierra Madre. But he was not through making headlines.

CHAPTER
SEVEN

COLUMBUS

In January 1916, the fragments of Villa's decimated Division of the North began to regroup in the mountains of Chihuahua. On January 10, Pablo López, one of Villa's officers, led an ambush that succeeded in capturing a train near Santa Ysabel. After robbing the Mexican passengers in the first car, López proceeded to the second and discovered that a group of North American mine operators were aboard, en route to Chihuahua City. With shouts of "¡Viva Villa!" López and his men proceeded to gun down the unarmed Americans as they sat in their seats or attempted to jump from the train and flee into the desert. Seventeen Americans died. The lone survivor of the massacre, who escaped by hiding in underbrush while his colleagues were murdered, provided chilling testimony of the incident to the North American and Mexican press.

Villa admitted ordering the attack on the train, but he denied authorizing López to harm U.S. citizens. It seems quite possible, considering the situation Villa was in at that time, that he may indeed have authorized the raid and massacre to provoke a breakdown in the newly harmonious relations between the Carranza government and the United States. If so, the gambit almost paid off. There were calls in the U.S. Congress for intervention in Mexico. But the Car-

Following his attack on Columbus, New Mexico, in 1916, Villa became a hated figure in the United States. Here he is hung in effigy at the annual Mummers' Parade in Philadelphia.

ranza government made a sincere effort to apprehend the culprits, and the United States was now becoming enmeshed in World War I. Moderate political elements in Congress prevailed. Several months later, Carranza's forces captured López, and he was sentenced to death. Shortly before his execution, he claimed that Villa had ordered the Santa Ysabel massacre.

Santa Ysabel marked an important turning point in U.S. relations with Pancho Villa. All references in the press to Villa as a modern-day Mexican Robin Hood ceased. The incident eliminated any possibility of Villa's obtaining political asylum. On Villa's part, the positive feelings he had toward the United States were replaced by bitterness at being held responsible for the actions of an enraged officer only nominally under his command. His desire for revenge became more important than his commitment to the Mexican Revolution.

The dissolution of his army, combined with the notoriety of the Santa Ysabel massacre, led Villa to adopt a desperate course of action. During the first week of March, he led the 500 men who still followed him to the border town of Las Palomas, Chihuahua, located just a few miles from Columbus, New Mexico. The commander of the American military garrison at Columbus received numerous reports that Villa planned to cross the border to attack Columbus, but since his information was not conclusive and was contradicted by other reports, he did not place his 300-man garrison on alert. There was reason to believe that Villa was in the area to begin a journey to Washington, where he hoped to convince the U.S. government to stop aiding Carranza. If that were the case, attacking Columbus was the last thing he would want to do.

On Monday, March 8, several newspapers in El Paso, Texas, reported that Villa, encamped near Las Palomas, had ordered the execution of two captured

North Americans. General John J. "Black Jack" Pershing, commander of the U.S. forces at Fort Bliss, was informed of this news and of Villa's alleged plan to attack Columbus. He had conflicting information that placed Villa in another area, poised to attack the Carranza garrison at Las Palomas. Pershing could not determine which reports to believe. Either way, there was little he could do. If he wished to reinforce Columbus, he would have had to seriously weaken other garrisons that were just as likely to be targets. Since Villa was moving along the border on the Mexican side of the line, there was no way that Pershing could obtain regular, reliable data about his location and intentions.

Villa soon resolved all doubts. At 4:00 A.M. on Tuesday, March 9, 1916, his men swooped into Columbus under the cover of darkness, firing in all directions and hurling torches into buildings. Shouts of "¡Viva Villa!" "¡Viva Mexico!" "¡Muerte [Death] a los Americanos!" and the moans of wounded men

Troopers of the 13th U.S. Cavalry survey the corpse of a Mexican raider after Villa's attack on Columbus. Villa's daring predawn raid might have succeeded in capturing the town if not for the bravery of a handful of U.S. soldiers, who held the attackers at bay until the rest of the garrison was awake.

shattered the predawn stillness. Within minutes, the undefended town was ablaze, and eight U.S. civilians lay dying, riddled with bullets.

Villa's men proceeded with such methodical precision through the buildings and streets of Columbus that it was clear they had scouted the city before the raid. They knew where to find cover from the garrison's machine guns, and they quickly located people who had access to cash and merchandise. The care they took to kill only men showed that Villa's followers were acting according to detailed orders.

Sixteen-year-old Arthur Ravel lived to tell what it was like to be in Columbus that morning. "We were in the Commercial Hotel building, and I seen Mrs. Ritchie, I think it was, in Mr. Walker's saloon, begging the Mexicans over there not to kill Mr. Ritchie. I heard one of the Mexicans; he said: 'Anything that looks like a white, kill him.' " After witnessing the murder of several other men that morning, Ravel was spared so that he could unlock his father's store. He vividly described the scene that took place as he walked up the street between two of Villa's men: "Bullets were flying in every direction; fires were going every place; you would see once in a while a man drop dead. I seen them loot our store and Mr. Walker's store, a hardware store, of saddles and so on, and hardware." Ravel escaped death only because the two Mexicans assigned to escort him were shot by townspeople.

Villa's carefully planned attack might have enabled him to capture Columbus, if not for the discipline and courage displayed by the U.S. troops. When the attack began, the only soldiers awake were a handful of sentries and a group of black cooks who were preparing breakfast. The cooks did not have any loaded rifles; all weapons and ammunition were kept locked in the armory for security. But when the shooting began, the cooks did not flee in panic. They fought back with the only weapons they had at hand—boiling water, kitchen knives, pots, and pans. Their courage and that of other soldiers who fought with clubs and with their bare hands bought the garrison just enough time. Before long, the rest of the troops were awake and fully armed.

The counterattack launched by the U.S. troops forced Villa to recall his men at dawn. Although the entire raid lasted little more than an hour, the physical and psychological devastation caused by the looting and fighting in Columbus's smoke-filled streets was massive. Many residents, fearing another assault and more atrocities, began fleeing the area on foot.

Villa left a small detachment to cover his retreat and galloped south with his men back into Mexico. The furious soldiers were not about to let Villa's men escape so easily. A pursuing column of 60 U.S. Cavalry overpowered the rear guard and rode into Mexico, pursuing the main force for eight hours. They fought several more skirmishes before lack of ammunition and exhaustion forced them to head back to Columbus.

Villa's men paid a high price for their leader's audacity—167 died, 13 were captured, and many more were wounded. Exactly why Villa decided to attack Columbus will never be known, but there are several possible motives: retaliation for U.S. aid to Carranza; obtaining badly needed supplies; punishing a merchant who had failed to deliver purchased ammunition; and creating a dispute between the Carranza and U.S. governments over the necessity of American military intervention.

From a military perspective, Villa's raid was a disaster: his casualties amounted to almost half his men. From a political perspective, however, it was a complete success. The U.S. response humiliated Carranza and restored Villa's prestige among the Mexican population.

Despite Carranza's refusal to authorize American intervention, the day after the raid President Wilson ordered the U.S. Army to retaliate. General Pershing organized a force that was determined to pursue Villa's band as far as necessary into Mexico, in order to capture it or destroy its ability to cause further trouble along the border.

The 3,000-man Punitive Expedition entered Mexico on March 15, 1916, in two distinct columns: one from Columbus and the other from Culberson's Ranch, which was located in the southwestern corner of New Mexico. Pershing ordered the mounted Culberson column to reach Colonia Dublán, a community of North American Mormons, within two days. He hoped that the column would arrive in time to protect the people living there from Villa's wrath, while also cutting off Villa's escape further south. The Culberson column accomplished its first goal but could not cut off Villa's retreat.

The second detachment of Pershing's forces arrived in Colonia Dublán three days later, on March 20. The following day, the united expedition moved deeper into Mexico. The long process of tracking down groups of Villa's scattered band began.

General John J. "Black Jack" Pershing, commander of U.S. forces at Fort Bliss, Texas, led 3,000 troops into Mexico in pursuit of Villa in March 1916. Thus the Columbus raid accomplished Villa's political objective—to drive a wedge between the United States and the Carranza regime, which strongly objected to Pershing's invasion.

Members of E Company of the 24th U.S. Infantry occupy trenches at Colonia Dublán, Mexico, in July 1916. The troops reached the city in time to protect its U.S. residents from Villa's wrath, but they were too late to prevent the bandit leader's escape into the mountains.

Villa utilized the six days between the Columbus raid and the arrival of the Culberson column in Colonia Dublán to disappear into the Chihuahua mountain wilderness he knew so well. Although he was sighted on several occasions and once was wounded below the left knee by a rifle shot, his pursuers, even with the aid of Apache Indian scouts, were never able to corner him. Because of Villa's ability to wriggle free repeatedly for 11 months while the Punitive Expedition's small, rapidly moving patrols searched for him, Mexicans turned him into a national folk hero.

The outrage of the Mexican public over the presence of Pershing's troops on the nation's soil presented Carranza with an impossible dilemma. While he wanted to see Villa captured, political necessities forced him to hamper the Punitive Expedition as much as possible. The longer the troops remained in Mexico and the farther south they advanced, the more hostile the population became. After Pershing's forces clashed with Mexican troops on two separate occasions, President Wilson was forced to mobilize the U.S. National Guard along the border to forestall attacks.

Considering the difficulties imposed upon the expedition by the need to supply 3,000 men in the rugged Sierra Madre wilderness, the lack of cooperation by the Carranza government, the wiliness of Villa, and the increasing animosity of the Mexican public, Pershing managed the situation with great skill. He never caught Villa, but he managed to pursue him for the better part of a year while avoiding a full-scale war with Mexico.

On September 1, 1916, Villa defied Pershing and resumed his guerrilla activities with a successful attack upon a Carranza military force near Satevo. Three weeks later he led a raid into Chihuahua City, obtaining a large supply of ammunition and freeing 1,600 prisoners from the penitentiary; most of them joined his band. On November 23, after three days of bitter fighting, Villa's men even expelled the Carranza garrison from Chihuahua City.

When Villa occupied Chihuahua on November 23, he did not attempt to restrain the behavior of his men. Numerous atrocities occurred, the most glaring being the systematic robbery and cold-blooded massacre of the city's Chinese population. Like most members of the peasantry, Villa despised the Chinese who had immigrated to Mexico. Their different appearance and customs, their dedication to establishing small businesses, and the rumors that they kept all their money hidden in their clothing made them tempting targets for Mexico's downtrodden peasants. Villa's men simply shot their Chinese victims on sight so that it would be easier to search them for money.

As if to demonstrate that Chihuahua was not an isolated case, the abuse of the Chinese community was repeated when Villa recaptured his old stronghold of Torreón on Christmas Eve. All other foreigners in the city were protected.

U.S. troops occupy one of the armed vehicles employed by the Punitive Expedition. Villa's knowledge of the rugged Sierra Madre enabled him to elude his pursuers for nearly a year, a feat that added to his legend as a Mexican folk hero.

By January 1917, it was obvious that the Punitive Expedition did not have enough men to eliminate Villa as a factor in Mexican affairs. Pershing stated that the only way he could accomplish his objective would be to beef up his forces and occupy northern Mexico. He knew the United States was not prepared for such a massive intervention. The nation's priorities had shifted from Mexico to Europe. Rather than starting a war with Mexico on the eve of U.S. involvement in World War I, President Wilson decided to order Pershing to withdraw his forces.

When the last U.S. troops crossed the border back into the United States on February 5, 1917, the responsibility for maintaining order in northern Mexico fell once again upon the soldiers of the Carranza government. Both Carranza and Villa welcomed the opportunity to square off yet again.

THE LAST CAMPAIGN

In April 1917, shortly after the United States declared war on Germany, Villa resumed attacking Carranza's garrisons near the U.S. border. On May 30, his men forced the garrison at Ojinaga to seek sanctuary on the American side of the border. However, this time Villa made no attempt to fortify and hold the town. Three days after capturing Ojinaga, he disappeared with his men into the mountain wilderness for the summer. The Ojinaga garrison quickly returned and reoccupied the town, only to be driven across the border by Villa again on November 15.

Throughout 1918, Villa continued to rebuild his army while conducting a series of raids against isolated Carranza garrisons. As soon as the fall harvest was completed, he attacked and looted Villa Ahumada, on the Juárez-Chihuahua railway. On December 12, he raided the mining community at Cusihuiriachic and seized $10,000 from the mining company safe. He also burned the company's woodpile. This, he said, was to force the company to buy more wood and thus create work for the people. A similar raid occurred on January 22, 1919, against another mining community at Santa Eulalia.

Villa during the final years of his military career, as he struggled to maintain his army and his prestige as a commander. Though he launched a number of successful raids between 1917 and 1918, the combined strength of the Carranza government and the United States finally forced him into retirement.

As his army and prestige grew once again, Villa's behavior changed. He once again adopted the behavior of a revolutionary guerrilla leader rather than just a bandit. He took the time to harangue the people during his raids, urging them to fight for their rights, and he was careful not to harm any North Americans or other foreigners. Once again, he could afford to be concerned about international public opinion.

By the spring of 1919, Villa commanded a well-equipped and well-trained striking force of over 1,500 men. On April 19, 1919, after a short battle, Villa recaptured Parral. To prevent negative publicity, he sealed off the city from journalists while his men looted over half a million dollars in gold from various companies' safes. The private property of foreigners was not touched, but Mexican dwellings were looted. Before he departed, Villa personally oversaw the execution of prisoners who had abandoned him to support Carranza.

The gold taken from Parral enabled Villa to pay his men, outfit new recruits, and purchase badly needed modern weapons and ammunition. His next goal in his carefully planned return to power was to obtain his old base of operations along the border, Ciudad Juárez.

A few minutes after midnight on June 14–15, Villa launched one of his classic nighttime attacks against the Juárez garrison. By 2:00 A.M., Villa's men had succeeded in driving the Carranza troops back into Fort Hidalgo. The battle seemed won, but then, shortly before dawn, the Carranza troops counterattacked and recaptured a substantial portion of the city.

After a morning respite, the fighting resumed. As soon as it became dark again, Villa ordered his men to take the offensive. The fighting became so intense that numerous shots by both sides began whizzing with considerable frequency into the U.S. side of the border. At approximately 11:00 P.M., after three soldiers and several women had been shot by stray bullets, the U.S. military commander in Juárez sent a gruff warning to Carranza's forces—"Get out of the way if you don't want to get hurt"—and ordered his men into the fray against Villa.

A lethal artillery barrage announced the U.S. decision. Hundreds of high-explosive shells rained down upon Villa's troops at the Juárez racetrack and throughout the city, as black U.S. infantrymen advanced en masse across the international bridge with fixed bayonets. Simultaneously, two columns of the Seventh Cavalry charged across the Rio Grande on a pontoon bridge to cut off the escape of Villa's men into the desert. The rout was complete. By dawn, the new army Villa had carefully nurtured for over two years had been annihilated.

Villa barely escaped the carnage in Juárez. He managed to avoid being captured by moving frequently and traveling with only a few loyal followers until he reached his old bandit hideout in the Chihua-

Led by an armored vehicle, U.S. troops of the 24th Cavalry occupy a section of Juárez, Mexico, in June 1919. A massive assault by U.S. artillery, infantry, and cavalry units on June 15 had effectively wiped out Villa's army and eliminated him as a force in Mexican politics.

hua mountains. His former ally, Emiliano Zapata, was not so fortunate. He was betrayed by one of his own officers for the reward offered by Carranza and was cut down by an assassin's bullet. At the close of 1919, Villa knew that it was only a matter of time until he suffered the same fate as Zapata, but he vowed that he would never surrender as long as Carranza held office.

Villa did not have to wait for long. After Carranza had become the constitutional president in May 1917, he did little to implement the basic reforms in land ownership, control of natural resources, and labor and social legislation that the radical Constitution of 1917 promised. Early in 1920, when Carranza tried to force the election of his chosen successor, he sealed his doom. Alvaro Obregón, the brilliant military strategist who had put him in office, came out of retirement to ensure his demise. Carranza waited too long to attempt his escape. Slowed down by the sacks of gold he attempted to steal from the treasury, he was captured and murdered in the mountains on his way to Veracruz on May 21, 1920.

Obregón proved to be an eloquent, sincere champion of the basic principles of the Mexican Revolution as expressed in the Constitution of 1917. Obregón's election to the presidency on December 1, 1920, after just a few months of interim rule by Adolfo de la Huerta, marked the beginning of the return to domestic order in Mexico after a decade of bloody social and political chaos.

With Carranza gone, Villa accepted the need to admit defeat. The terms his old enemy offered were extremely generous: Villa was allowed to retain the rank of general with full pay, and as a reward for his past services to the revolution, he was granted ownership of the magnificent 25,000-acre Rancho del Canutillo.

Alvaro Obregón, who had lost his right arm while defeating Villa at the Battle of Aguascalientes in 1915, became president of Mexico in December 1920. One of Mexico's finest leaders, Obregón was capable of treating former enemies with great generosity: he permitted Villa to retain his military privileges and granted him a large estate.

Retired at the age of 43, Villa threw himself into improving the productivity of his new property and modernizing the nearby city of Parral, showing the same energy he had employed to build his famous Division of the North. The generous pension he received and the profits from carefully managing his hacienda enabled him to purchase mechanized equipment and the talents of agricultural experts.

In his relations with his family and workers he epitomized the stereotype of the retired military com-

mander and benevolent despot. He resumed living
with his legitimate wife, María Luz, and sent his two
youngest sons to a private boarding school in Texas.
For his workers' children, he built a school on the
ranch and hired a teacher.

Villa seemed to genuinely enjoy his new life of
tranquility and apparently harbored no ill will toward
anyone. He entertained numerous Mexicans, Europeans, and North Americans at his ranch. Once, in
a chance encounter with a North American on a
railway journey, he let the man handle his famous
pearl-handled revolvers and even showed off the
scars on his left leg, where he had been wounded by
Pershing's men.

Family life at Canutillo was good but insecure.
There were too many people in Mexico whose rela-
tives had died because of Pancho Villa, and there were
many people in high places who feared that he might
not remain retired. As long as Villa lived, the threat of
domestic turmoil in northern Mexico remained. Before long, Villa's enemies raised about $50,000 to
finance his assassination.

Villa, always wild about automobiles, had taken to
riding around in a Dodge sedan. On Friday, July 20,
1923, while driving home from Parral with his bodyguards, Villa noticed a street vendor waving to him at
an intersection. He slowed his car to return the greet-
ing, and the vendor shouted, "¡Viva Villa!" The shout
was the signal for a squad of gunmen concealed in a
house by the roadside. Raising their rifles, the assassins
opened fire on the Dodge, which swerved off the road
and crashed into a tree. Villa died instantly, riddled by
seven bullets. Four of his bodyguards perished with
him.

Several months later, Jesús Salas Barrazas, the congressman for the El Oro district of Durango and a
supporter of Obregón whom Villa had once pistol-
whipped in a dispute over a woman, was arrested and

charged with the murder. He claimed innocence but was convicted and sentenced to 20 years in prison. He actually served only six months. Shortly before his death in 1951 in Mexico City, Barrazas confessed to being one of the seven men who had ambushed Villa.

Villa was buried in the Parral cemetery, but even in death he found no peace. Grave robbers desecrated the tomb in 1926 and removed his head, which was never recovered.

In surveying Villa's life, it is often difficult to separate fact from legend. To his critics, Villa's career as a bandit before the revolution proves that he was guilty of all the crimes attributed to him. The critics believe that he was nothing more than a pathological killer whose avowed commitment to revolutionary reforms was only a cover for murder. To his supporters, Villa was the epitome of the peasant rebel, a man who lacked education but possessed high ideals and a keen intelligence. According to

Villa and one of his bodyguards, Colonel Trillo, lie dead in Villa's Dodge sedan after an ambush on July 20, 1923. Jesús Salas Barrazas, a congressman who took part in the assassination, was sentenced to 20 years in prison for the crime but served only six months.

Villa's admirers, he killed in order to survive, but he always remained true to his commitment to the redistribution of the nation's wealth.

The common people of northern Mexico sought and found in Pancho Villa a deliverer who wreaked vengeance upon the hacienda overlords and mine owners they could not reach. Villa was a hero to them because many of his extraordinary deeds, both generous and vicious, seemed typical of his origin as a member of the peasantry. The inability of the powerful U.S. Army to catch him made him a symbol of the Mexican peasant's ability to endure in the face of overwhelming odds.

One thing is clear. Villa did not join the revolution in 1910 for personal profit. Instead of hoarding the plunder he obtained as a rebel officer, he used it to pay his men and to purchase military equipment. Financially, he would have gained a great deal more by continuing to pursue his life as a bandit.

Villa's bullet-riddled body lies in the hospital at Parral, awaiting an autopsy. Historians continue to debate Villa's place in Mexican history, but to the people of northern Mexico he remains a folk hero who fought for the rights of the underdog.

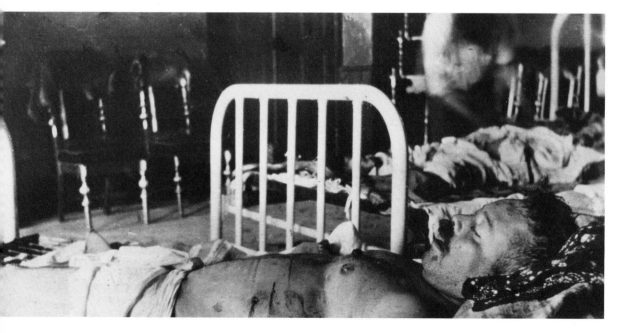

Villa probably became a revolutionary because of his experiences as a young man. Revenge for the abuse he had been forced to endure and a desire to protect other poor Mexicans from the same fate were undoubtedly important factors. In his loyalty to Francisco Madero and his dedication to the revolution's reform program he remained, in his own unique way, steadfast throughout his life.

Shortly before his death, Villa proudly explained to a visiting journalist that he had established the little school on his ranch because he realized that guns and violence would never lead to social reform. "I fought for ten years so that poor men could live like human beings. . . . But it wasn't much use. . . . Nothing much can be done at all until the common people are educated."

Few figures in modern Mexican history have maintained a stronger hold on the masses than Pancho Villa. It was the irony of his life that he was betrayed by a street vendor, a member of the class from which he sprang and for whose cause he had always expressed devotion.

CHRONOLOGY

1878	Born Doroteo Arango in Rio Grande, Mexico, on June 5
1894	Adopts the name Francisco "Pancho" Villa and joins an outlaw gang; spends much of the next 16 years as a bandit
1909	Marries María Luz Corral
1910	Mexicans revolt against the regime of Porfirio Díaz; Villa joins the revolutionary army with the rank of captain
1911	Villa's troops capture Ciudad Juárez; first phase of the Mexican Revolution ends with the overthrow of Díaz; Francisco I. Madero elected president of Mexico
1912	Villa defends Madero government from attempted coup; condemned to death for disobeying orders; sentence is commuted to two years in prison; Villa escapes and flees to El Paso, Texas
1913	Madero assassinated; Victoriano Huerta assumes the office of president; Villa vows to avenge Madero and joins anti-Huerta alliance; captures Juárez and Chihuahua, becoming the master of northern Mexico and an international celebrity

1914   U.S. forces occupy Mexican port of Veracruz, putting pressure on Huerta regime; Villa's army captures Zacatecas; Huerta resigns; Venustiano Carranza becomes provisional president; Villa breaks with Carranza and forms alliance with peasant leader Emiliano Zapata; Villa and Zapata capture Mexico City

1915   Villa withdraws from Mexico City to battle pro-Carranza forces in the north; suffers crushing defeats at the hands of General Obregón in battles at Celaya and Aguascalientes; United States recognizes Carranza regime as the legitimate government of Mexico and cuts off aid to Villa; Villa suffers another defeat at Agua Prieta

1916   Villa's forces raid Columbus, New Mexico, looting the town and killing U.S. citizens

1916–17   3,000 U.S. troops pursue Villa unsuccessfully through the mountains of northern Mexico

1918   Villa regroups his army and resumes his attacks on Carranza's forces

1919   Villa's attack on Juárez ends in disaster as his army is destroyed by intervening U.S. troops

1920   Carranza's regime collapses; Obregón is elected president of Mexico, ending the 10-year Mexican Revolution; Villa accepts pension and estate from Obregón and becomes a rancher

1923   Assassinated in Parral, Mexico, on July 20

FURTHER READING

Atkin, Ronald. *Revolution! Mexico, 1910–1920.* New York: John Day, 1970.

Braddy, Haldeen. *The Paradox of Pancho Villa.* El Paso: Texas Western Press, 1978.

Brenner, Anita. *The Wind That Swept Mexico.* Austin: University of Texas Press, 1971.

Clendenen, Clarence C. *The United States and Pancho Villa: A Study in Unconventional Diplomacy.* Ithaca: Cornell University Press, 1961.

Cockcroft, James. *Mexico.* New York: Monthly Review Press, 1990.

Guzmán, Martín Luis. *Memoirs of Pancho Villa.* Translated and abridged by Virginia Taylor. Austin: University of Texas Press, 1965.

Hall, Linda B. *Revolution on the Border: The United States and Mexico, 1910–1920.* Albuquerque: University of New Mexico Press, 1988.

Johnson, William Weber. *Heroic Mexico: The Narrative History of a Twentieth-Century Revolution.* San Diego: Harcourt Brace Jovanovich, 1984.

Justice, Glenn. *Revolution on the Rio Grande: Mexican Raids and Army Pursuits, 1916–1919.* El Paso: Texas Western Press, 1992.

Machado, Manuel A. *Centaur of the North: Francisco Villa, the Mexican Revolution, and Northern Mexico.* Austin: Eakin Press, 1988.

Peterson, Jessie, and Thelma Cox Knoles, eds. *Pancho Villa: Intimate Recollections by People Who Knew Him.* New York: Hastings House, 1977.

Ragan, John. *Emiliano Zapata.* New York: Chelsea House, 1989.

Reed, John. *Insurgent Mexico.* New York: Simon & Schuster, 1969.

Soto, Shirlene Ann. *The Mexican Woman: A Study of Her Participation in the Revolution, 1910–1940.* Palo Alto: R & E Research Associates, 1979.

Torres, Elias L. *Twenty Episodes in the Life of Pancho Villa.* Translated by Sheila M. Ohlendorf. Austin: Encino Press, 1973.

Womack, John J. *Zapata and the Mexican Revolution.* New York: Knopf, 1969.

INDEX

STEVEN O'BRIEN taught high school social studies in Massachusetts for nearly 20 years. He holds an M.A. in history from the University of Connecticut as well as a certificate of advanced study and a Ph.D. from Harvard University. His writing has appeared in the *New York Times Magazine* and other publications, and he is the author of *Antonio López de Santa Anna* in the Chelsea House HISPANICS OF ACHIEVEMENT series. He is currently headmaster at the American Community School of Athens in Greece.

RODOLFO CARDONA is professor of Spanish and comparative literature at Boston University. A renowned scholar, he has written many works of criticism, including *Ramón, a Study of Gómez de la Serna and His Works* and *Visión del esperpento: Teoría y práctica del esperpento en Valle-Inclán.* Born in San José, Costa Rica, he earned his B.A. and M.A. from Louisiana State University and received a Ph.D. from the University of Washington. He has taught at Case Western Reserve University, the University of Pittsburgh, the University of Texas at Austin, the University of New Mexico, and Harvard University.

JAMES COCKCROFT is currently a visiting professor of Latin American and Caribbean studies at the State University of New York at Albany. A three-time Fulbright scholar, he earned a Ph.D. from Stanford University and has taught at the University of Massachusetts, the University of Vermont, and the University of Connecticut. He is the author or coauthor of numerous books on Latin American subjects, including *Neighbors in Turmoil: Latin America, The Hispanic Experience in the United States: Contemporary Issues and Perspectives,* and *Outlaws in the Promised Land: Mexican Immigrant Workers and America's Future.*